~ ~ ~

CHOICES

~ ~ ~

Mia N. Jones

CHOICES
Mia N. Jones

Published By:
The "LIGHT" Designs Book Publishers
(*a division of Kingdom Publishing Group, Inc.*)
P.O. Box 505, Ashland, VA 23005
804-515-9100

Library of Congress
©June, 2006 by Mia N. Jones
ISBN: 0-9772964-5-8

Cover design: Matthew Williams, Sr.

Unless otherwise noted, scripture quotations taken from the King James Version of the Bible.

Printed in the United States of America

Deuteronomy 30:19

I call heaven and earth as witnesses today
against you that I have set before you
life and death, blessings and cursing;
therefore choose life that both you
and your descendants may live.

~ SHOUT OUTS ~
(acknowledgements and "thank yous")

I would like to show some love to...

God

My Parents, Pastors Keith and Carla Jones

My Grandparents

My Sisters

My Aunts and Uncles and

All My Family

Mrs. Dietrich (My Editor)

Mrs. Cousin

Blair Starks

Kam Fields

Dee

Chante (Best friend)

Terry Harris

Aarian

The Johnson's

The Washington's

The Graves'

Now Faith That Works Church

New Light Church

All My Friends

Everybody who supported me.

~ TABLE OF CONTENTS ~

~ INTRODUCTION ~

CHOICES is a riveting story about two teens, Shakia and Quincy, who are faced with very important life decisions that will determine the outcome of their futures. Not only will they experience intense pressure from their peers, but they also have to deal with problems they are having at home.

Shakia is a straight "A" student in high school. Her father is the head Pastor of a church and her mom is a Real Estate Agent. She has three great friends whom she has known since middle school. But, although her life appears to be in order, Shakia still believes something is missing...

Quincy is a senior in high school. He is the school's best basketball player and is working on getting a college basketball scholarship. At home, he has to contend with a dad who is an alcoholic and who complains about everything. What makes it even worse is that Quincy constantly witnesses his mom going through verbal abuse from his dad. Quincy feels he needs to be what other people want him to be...

The stories of Shakia and Quincy are symbolic of the lives and challenges many young people face every day. As you journey through the pages of CHOICES, you will be amazed, enlightened, and sometimes frightened at the decisions these young people and their friends make. Their choices will change their lives forever...

~ Chapter One~

CHANGES...

CHANGES...

"Shakia come down here for dinner." her mom called. "I'll be down in a minute," she answered. Shakia threw clothes from her closet trying to find an outfit for the party.

"Shakia, I'm not going to call you again." Shakia ran down the stairs and sat down at the table.

"Why did I have to call you for dinner two times?"

"Sorry. I was on the phone with Sidney; we were talkin' 'bout our project." Her mom looked at her watch and then at the door. "Where is your dad? This is the third time he has missed dinner. Oh well, say grace."

"Lord, bless this food we're about to eat and let it have no hurt, harm, or danger to our bodies in Jesus' name. Amen."

"So, how was your day at school?"

Shakia looked at her plate, then at her mom. "It was fine." She took a deep breath, looked out the window and said, "Mom, if I wanted to go to a party would you let me go?"

Shakia's mom sighed and looked at her and declared, "You know there is nothing at those parties but trouble and you already know what my answer will be."

Shakia looked at her plate again and began to play with her food. After she finished eating she went to her room, finished picking out her outfit, and then began to do her homework. Her mom came in her room and sat on her bed.

"Shakia, I trust that you will make good choices while you are in high school." Shakia looked at her mom and replies, "I will. My main focus is goin' to college."

"That's what I wanted to hear. Well, good night. It's eleven o'clock; I'm going to sleep." When her mom left she looked at her clock and wondered if Jalissa was going to call her. Time passed and soon it was twelve o'clock, and Shakia began to give up hope. A few minutes later her cell phone rang.

"Hello," she answered.

"Hey, this is Jalissa. What street do you live on?"

"I live on Deer Park, 2631."

"I will be there in ten minutes, are you ready?"

"Yeah, but when you get to my house don't honk the horn. I will be outside." Jalissa said "Ok." Shakia hustled to put on her clothes, opened her window and climbed out.

~ ~ ~ ~ ~ ~ ~ ~

"Yo, Quincy this shorty wants to holla at you." Deon'te said. Quincy looked around and walked into the kitchen. He sat down at the table and put his head down.

"Yo, Quincy are you straight man?"

"I'll be in there in a minute." Soon he got up from the table and went back to the party. Before he knew it, he was drinking and dancing.

"Quincy, you need to chill out with all that drinkin'," Ricky told him. "Man, I know what I'm doin' and I'm not even drunk. Don't worry about me." He drank so much he began to kiss a girl and soon took her upstairs. When they went upstairs, he was looking for a room to enter. After he found a room he sat on the bed and the girl began to approach him as she unbuttoned her shirt. The girl made her way to him and laid on top of him and they began to kiss.

"Boom!"

"Quincy what are you doin'?" Ricky yelled. He slammed the door open, stormed in the room and led Quincy out and then down the stairs. "I'm 'bout to take you home," Ricky exclaimed. Ricky led him out of the house and took Quincy's car keys. They got in the car and started on their way home. "What were you thinkin'? Ricky asked. I know you're drunk. I thought you could handle your liquor better than that."

"I was 'bout to hit that and you want to come in like some Superman hero." answered Quincy.

Ricky pulled the car over and lectured, "You know those hoe's don't give a care 'bout you. They're lookin' to get you caught." Quincy looked at Ricky with a drunken look on his face and babbled, "I knew what I was doin'."

Ricky glanced at him with a strange look on his face. "What do you mean you knew what you were doin'? That girl coulda' gotten pregnant, she coulda' had somethin', and you talkin' 'bout you knew what you were doin'! You drunk and you had no clue what you were doin'." Quincy turned over in the seat and went to sleep. Ricky began to pray for him, "God, please bless Quincy. Help him make good choices." When Ricky pulled up to Quincy's driveway it was 12:30 in the morning. He woke him up and helped him into the house.

As they stumbled to his room, Quincy asked, "Can you tell me about it tomorrow mornin' because you know I'm not gonna remember." He looked at his drunken friend and nodded, then he laid him in the bed.

Ricky laid on the floor, turned on his back and began to pray again, "Lord, I know I come to you a lot. Please help Quincy to see all the tricks of the enemy and continue to bless him with your mercy and grace in Jesus' name. Amen."

~ ~ ~ ~ ~ ~ ~ ~

Shakia looked at her watch and then down the street. She saw car lights coming towards her house and she began to get excited. But then she looked at the car and noticed it was her dad pulling into the driveway. She ran towards the side of the house so her dad wouldn't see her. As her dad got out of the car she noticed another car coming down the street. Her dad went into the house and she ran towards her ride. After she got in the car she noticed an unusual smell.

"What's that smell?" she asked. "Those are Black and Milds," Jalissa answered. "They smell good," Shakia replied.

Shakia looked out of the car window and began to think to herself, "I can't believe I snuck out of the house on a school night." "Shakia, you want a Black?" asked Mercedes. She thought to herself for a second. "No, I'm straight. My mom might smell it on me or in my clothes," she explained. The girls looked at each other and laughed.

"Look Kia, do you care if I call you Kia?" Jalissa asked. "No, that's fine," Shakia said. "Don't worry 'bout that," said Jalissa, "we have a solution to that problem."

Jalissa pulled into a gas station and told Shakia to come in with her. Jalissa went to the trunk of her car and got some clothes out. They walked in the gas station and Jalissa handed some clothes to Shakia and told her to change. She walked into the bathroom and looked at the skirt and shirt she had to put on. As she began to change clothes she looked at herself with a smile. "Yo, Kia hurry up." Shakia folded her clothes and opened the bathroom door.

"Now that's sexy, the boys are gonna be all over you." Jalissa started to walk out of the door and stopped to look around. She took two packs of gum and walked out of the door. When they got outside she tossed Shakia a pack of gum.

"Dang, you look good, girl. I shoulda wore somethin' like that," Ashley announced. Once they got in the car, Shakia felt good about herself and wanted to be just like Jalissa.

"Hey, Jalissa. I'll take that Black now." Jalissa looked at Shakia with a smile and handed her a lighter and a black. She lit the Black and took a puff. She began to cough. Jalissa and the other girls laughed.

"You'll get used to it," Jalissa exclaimed. "Yeah, it took me a while to get used to it too," Ashley said. Mercedes looked at Shakia with an annoyed look on her face. Shakia noticed she was looking at her and wondered why.

"We're here," Jalissa shouted. Shakia got out of the car and saw all the upper classman dancing, drinking, and smoking.

She threw her black on the ground and put it out. As they were walking towards the door, a boy grabbed Shakia by her wrist. She was so surprised she snatched away.

"My bad, shorty, I just wanted to holla at you," he said hesitantly. Jalissa walked up to the boy and interrupted, "She don't talk to scrubs, so find ya'self a lil hoe to talk to." He stared at them for a second, then gave them the finger and walked off.

"You can do better than that man hoe," Jalissa told her. "I didn't know what to do." Shakia replied. "Don't worry. Just stay with me, and watch what I do."

"Ight." Jalissa and Shakia walked into the party.

There was music Shakia had never heard before. She was in awe. Ashley walked up to Shakia and gave her a drink.

"What's this?"

"It's ginger ale mixed with Vodka." Shakia looked at her drink and took a deep breath and began to drink. She started to cough and choke. "My chest burns," she cried. "It's supposed to," Ashley replied. "Don't worry you just a virgin to this."

Shakia started looking at everyone dancing and having a good time and she thought of how she had never danced in front of people before. She went to lean against the wall, and she saw Jalissa flirting with a boy. Shakia watched closely and took note of what Jalissa was doing. She took another sip of her drink and coughed and she noticed that a boy was looking at her from across the room. He started to make his way to her and the closer he got, the more nervous she got. "Hey, how you doin' ma?"

She looked over at Jalissa and waited for the nod. As Jalissa gave her the nod, she replied, "I'm fine. How 'bout you?"

"I'm straight, so what's yo name?"

"Shakia." He started to move closer to her.

"What's ya name?"

"My boys call me JJ."

Shakia became more nervous as the boy moved even closer to her. He began to whisper in her ear. "How 'bout you and me go upstairs for a lil bit." When he said that, all she could think about was what her mom told her before she went to bed, ... *"Shakia, I trust that you will make good choices while you are in high school."*

... He took her by the hand and led her up the stairs and then into the game room. After they sat down on the couch, he started to touch her leg and kiss her neck. Shakia didn't know what to do or even how to react. Then he lifted her shirt. "Can you go get me another drink?" she quickly asked. He looked annoyed and slowly got up and went downstairs.

While he was gone, her mom's words were still running through her mind. Minutes passed and he came back with the drink. She took it and drank it right away. All of a sudden she began to get light-headed. She started laughing and talking about nothing. While she was laughing, the boy began to slip his hand up her skirt and continued to kiss her on her neck. She was so drunk she was clueless to what was going on.

"Bang Bang" came from downstairs!
The boy jumped up and went to look out the door. Jalissa ran up the stairs yelling, "They shootin'!" Jalissa ran into the room, grabbed Shakia by the arm and ran downstairs. Everyone downstairs was running towards the door. Jalissa saw the crowd of people and went to the kitchen and ran out the back door. They ran to the front of the house.

"Where are they?" Jalissa asked. They started walking down the street. Shakia couldn't even walk straight.

"Honk Honk!" It was Ashley and Mercedes. "Get in the car hurry-up!" Mercedes shrieked. Shakia stumbled trying to get in the car as Jalissa pushed her. After they drove away everyone started laughing. "Kia, you was doin' ya thing tonight," Jalissa said.

15

Shakia was so messed up she fell asleep in the car. "Jalissa, are you sure she's not goin' to slow us down?" Mercedes asked. "Naw, stop sweatin'. We'll get her just like we got you." Ashley indicated. "What you mean just like you got me?" Mercedes shrieked.

"Man, don't listen to her, she's just playin' with you," Jalissa concluded. They pulled up to Shakia's house. "Kia, you home. Wake up!" Jalissa yelled. She slowly woke up, opened the car door, and fell out. She got up slowly and sat on the curb.

"Yo, Kia see you tomorrow and, oh yeah, sit with us at lunch," Jalissa replied. She nodded and started walking towards her bedroom window. When she got in her room she looked at her clock. It was 3:45 in the morning and she still had school the next day. Suddenly, Shakia passed out on her bed.

<u>Deception - 1 Corinthians 15:33,34</u> - *"Do not be deceived: Evil company corrupts good habits. Awake to righteousness, and do not sin; for some do not have the knowledge of God. I speak this to your shame."*

<u>Drinking - Romans 13:13</u> - *"Let us walk properly, as in the day, not in revelry and drunkenness, not in lewdness and lust, not in strife and envy."*

~ Chapter Two~

LUNCH TIME...

LUNCH TIME

"Shakia, time to get up!" her mom yelled from downstairs. Shakia rolled over in her bed and pulled the pillow over her head. Her mom began to hit the ceiling with a broom.

"I'm getting up!" She got out of the bed and went to the bathroom. When she looked in the mirror, she still had the clothes on that Jalissa gave her. She ran back to her room and shut her door. She hurried and took the clothes off and threw them under the bed.

"Shakia, you're running late. Hurry up!" She ran in the bathroom and hopped in the shower. While she was in the shower she thought about what she did last night and how much fun it was. She got out of the shower and rushed to get dressed. She grabbed her book bag and ran down the stairs.

"Bye, mom. I can't eat. I'm goin' to miss the bus."

"Hold on, sweetie, I'll take you to school. I fixed breakfast for you." Shakia sat down at the table and started to eat. "Slow down, honey. What's the rush?"

Shakia looked up from her plate and smiled. "I just wanted to hurry and get to school so I can see Sidney's project."

"Sweetie, why are your eyes so red? Did you sleep ok last night?" She paused for a second, "Umm, I kept wakin' up from bad dreams."

"Well you know what to do when you have dreams like that, don't you?"

"Yeah, I know. Pray and ask God for sweet sleep."

"You got it. Now get your stuff together so we can get out of here." Shakia grabbed her things and went to get into the car. As they were driving, her mom started talking to her. "Shakia if something was going on with you, you would tell me wouldn't you?"

"Of course, who else would help me get through it?"
They pulled up to the front of the school and Shakia got out.

"Do you want me to pick you up?"

"No, I'll catch a ride from Sidney's mom."

"Ok."

Her mom drove away and Shakia walked into the school. When she walked past the library, Sidney was standing by a pole waiting for her. "Hey Shakia, why didn't you call me last night?" Sidney asked. "I got in trouble with my mom and she took my phone, but I got it back."

"Oh, so do you want to stay the night at my house tonight?"

"I can't. My mom wants me to do somethin' for her."

"Ok, maybe next weekend."

While they were walking to class Shakia saw Jalissa and the girls. As she passed them, Jalissa called her over. "Hold on, Sidney." She walked over to Jalissa. "So are you goin' to eat lunch with us today?"

"Yeah, but I have to go to class so I'll holla at you later."

Shakia turned around and walked back over to Sidney. "What was that all about?" she asked.

"She just wanted me to baby-sit tonight." As they walked to class, Shakia started to feel bad for lying to her friend.

Toni saw Shakia walking down the hallway, "Hey Shakia, why you didn't call anybody last night?" Toni asked.

"I got in trouble and my mom took my phone." They walked into class and sat at their desk.

~ ~ ~ ~ ~ ~ ~ ~

"Yo, Quincy, you missed it last night? They started shootin' at the party," Deon'te said.

"Good thing my man Ricky got me out of there." replied Quincy.

While they were talking, Ricky walked in the lunchroom. "What's up ya'll?" he said.

Deon'te looked at Ricky with a mean scowl on his face.

"Hey, Ricky, thanks for last night. I owe you." Quincy said. "Don't worry 'bout it, just make better choices. Plus I don't want you to mess up your career."

"Yo, Quincy, I'll holla at you later," Deon'te said. Ricky watched him walk away. "Why was ya man muggin' me?" he asked. "I don't know, he's not a threat," Quincy said. They got their lunches and sat at their table. While they were eating, Ricky was thinking about what happened at the party. "Quincy, do you remember what happened last night?" Quincy looked at Ricky with a questioning look. "Naw, what happened? All I remember is dancin' and havin' a couple of drinks."

"You did more than that; you went upstairs with the school hoe." Quincy put his head on the table and asked, "What I do?"

"You ain't do anything 'cause I walked in and stopped you."

"See, you always watchin' out for me." said Quincy gratefully. Ricky looked away and saw Deon'te glaring at him, then he turned back to Quincy and said, "I'm not always goin' to be there for you. If you keep hangin' with people like Deon'te you goin' to end up in jail somewhere."

Quincy looked at his watch and then at a girl sitting across the lunch room. Ricky continued to lecture Quincy and soon he noticed that he wasn't listening. Ricky got up from the table and left him sitting there. When Quincy turned around to talk to Ricky, he was gone. Quincy got up from the table and heard, "Don't worry 'bout that man he's just a church boy," Deon'te said.

"Don't talk 'bout my man like that; he's just tryin' to help me."

"Help you; he's tryin' to stop you. You're supposed to live life to the fullest, like everyday is your last. You don't know what may happen tomorrow." Deon'te glanced at the girl Quincy was looking at.

"So if I was you I would go holla at that."

Quincy looked at Deon'te and then started to walk towards the girl. While all this was going on, Ricky was watching from afar. He walked off and started to talk to God.

"Lord, why can't he see the traps Deon'te is puttin' in front of him? How do I get through to him? What do I do? I feel like I can't help him. Give me some kind of answer."

Ricky walked back to the lunch room and saw that Quincy was still talking to the girl. He sat at the table and waited for lunch to end.

~ ~ ~ ~ ~ ~ ~ ~

"Shakia, hurry up, we're goin' to be late for lunch!" Whitney yelled. Shakia got up from her desk and ran towards the door. The four girls walked towards the lunchroom. On their way to lunch, Sidney saw a boy walking down the hallway.

"Who is that? He's fine."

Toni watched the boy walk past and said, "Oh, his name is Ricky. He's real cool with the star of the basketball team, Quincy."

"Well, he looks extra good ..." Sidney replied.

Shakia started to laugh, "He don't want no lil tenth grader."

"Girl, what you talkin' 'bout? I look good," Sidney said. They continued to the lunchroom. Shakia started to walk ahead of the group.

"Why are you walkin' so fast?" Whitney asked. Shakia continued to walk quickly.

"I have to go to the bathroom." She continued to the bathroom while her friends went to lunch. When she got into the bathroom, she stared at herself in the mirror with a worried look on her face. "How am I gonna pull this off," she thought to herself.

Jalissa walked into the bathroom, "Are you worried 'bout ya lil friends?" Shakia turned around and looked surprised. "A lil bit, I don't know what to tell them." Jalissa moved closer and put her hand on Shakia's shoulder. "Just tell them I needed to talk to you 'bout somethin'."

Shakia looked away. "I don't like lyin' to them."

Jalissa looked Shakia in the eyes and said, "Stop sweatin' over them. I got you." They walked out of the bathroom and went to the cafeteria. Shakia was looking for her friends and saw that they were still in the lunch line. So she went and sat with Jalissa and the girls.

"Hey Kia," they said. Mercedes looked at Shakia and rolled her eyes. "So ladies, what's the plan for tonight?" Ashley asked. "It's Friday. You know we have to go to the mall to pick out an outfit for a party tonight," Jalissa replied. Shakia noticed that her friends were seated and eating lunch.

"You comin' out with us, Kia?" Ashley asked. She looked at the girls and smiled. "Yeah, but I don't know how my mom is goin' to let me go."

"Just tell her you stayin' at one of ya lil friend's house," Jalissa suggested. Shakia looked over at her friends and then turned back to her new friends. "Aight, I'll see if that will work. If not I will call you."

They all got up from the table to throw their lunch away. Shakia noticed her friends saw her with Jalissa. She tried to hide behind the three girls. "What you doin', Kia?" Mercedes asked. "Nothin'."

"Oh, you doin' somethin, what-you don't want your lil friends to see you with us?"

The girls walked out of the lunch room and towards the gym. "Where we goin'?" Shakia asked. "We're goin' to the mall," Jalissa answered.

"You mean now... durin' school?"

"Yeah, why you stressin'?"

"No, I just thought we were goin' after school." Ashley and Mercedes glanced at each and started to laugh. "Well, I'm goin' to give you two options. Either come to the mall with us or stay at school and learn ya lil school lessons," Jalissa said.

Shakia stopped walking and thought for a second. She then looked back at Jalissa. "Let's go," she said. They walked out of the school and ran towards Jalissa's car. The girls got into the car and sped off.

"Kia, why you roll with those lil school nerds?" Jalissa asked. "Well we've been friends since seventh grade."

"What if I asked you to start rollin' with us?"

"I would be down for whatever." Jalissa turned and smiled at her with a friendly smile. It was fifth period when they arrived at the mall. Shakia was worried about what she was missing in history class, but she continued on with her new friends. They walked around until they found the right store. They walked into Urban City and Shakia's eyes widened when she saw some of the clothes. There were skirts and shorts three inches long. She had always wanted to look like the girls on the videos.

"Kia, find you some clothes cause the lil school girl look is played out and you want boys to be on you, not runnin' from you," Ashley said. "Yeah, the lil school girl look gets no play at all," Mercedes added.

She looked down at her clothes and then looked at what Jalissa was wearing. Jalissa was carrying a big purse-like bag on her arm. "Jalissa, can you come here for a second?" Shakia asked.

As Jalissa made her way to Shakia, she stopped to look at a shirt. She looked to see if the store owner was looking and she stuffed the shirt in her bag and walked off. Shakia was shocked at what she had seen.

Jalissa walked up to Shakia and said, "What's up?" "I don't have any money to buy anything."

"Neither do I. This store doesn't have an alarm. Trust me I've done this fifty million times. Hurry and pick out some outfits and put them in my bag." Shakia looked around to see if anyone was looking. She grabbed the clothes and put them in the bag. "You know you're goin' to need shoes with that, right?" Jalissa said. Shakia walked over towards the shoe section and saw these cute open toed shoes. "Jalissa, come here."

She made her way to Shakia who threw the shoes in the bag, then walked out of the store. When she got outside the store, she sat on the bench and thought about what her mom said. "Why did you run out of the store like that?" Jalissa asked. "I didn't see anything else I wanted." Shakia replied

Ashley and Mercedes walked up behind Jalissa with purses on their arms also. "Next time bring a bag of ya own so you can get some more stuff," Ashley suggested.

The girls walked around the mall until they were ready to go. Shakia looked at the clock in the car and saw that school was almost over. "Kia, I'm goin' to take you home. Ask ya mom if you can stay at one of ya old friend's house," Jalissa said.

"What 'bout my clothes?" she asked.

"Take 'em and put 'em in the back of ya closet or somethin'."

"What time are you goin' to pick me up?"

"I'll be there around ten." Jalissa pulled up to Shakia's house and opened the door with stolen clothes in her hand.

Decisions (peer pressure) - Ezekiel 11:12
And you shall know that I am the Lord; for you have not walked in My statues nor executed My judgments, but have done according to the customs of the Gentiles which are all around you.

~ Chapter Three~

LET'S PARTY...

LET'S PARTY...

"Shakia, I'm home," her mom yelled from downstairs. Shakia was in her room when she heard her mom's voice. She threw all the stolen clothes in the back of the closet.

"Hey, mom." She walked out of her room and went downstairs. "How was your day?" her mom asked.

"It was like always."

"I have to go with your dad tonight. He's preaching at a church and I have to be there."

"Well, can I stay at Sidney's house tonight? Her mom already said it was ok." Her mom paused for a second and sat on the couch. "Did you do your homework?"

"Yeah, when I got home."

"Alright, I guess you can."

Shakia thanked her mom and ran up the stairs. When she got in her room, she laid on the bed and said, "I can't believe I'm doin this." All of a sudden her phone rang. "Hello," she answered. "This is Sidney. What happened to you today at lunch? You disappeared." Shakia didn't know what to say. "Umm, my mom came and picked me up for a doctor's appointment." It was an odd silence on the phone. "Then why were you with those girls? You didn't even sit with us at lunch." "They had to talk to me 'bout somethin'." Shakia said. She started to worry that Sidney was getting suspicious. "Well, I have to go to church with my mom so I will call you back later tonight," Shakia lied.

She hung up the phone before Sidney could even say anything. Shakia started to get ready for her Friday night party. As she was packing, she found a Black and Mild in her book bag. She took it out of her bag and placed it on top of her dresser. Shakia continued to pack her clothes and when she finished she lay on her bed and thought about her new friends. She thought about the stolen clothes, the smoking, and drinking at the party. A few minutes later she went to her dresser and stared at the black. She picked it up and put it in her pants pocket. Shakia walked out of her room and went downstairs. She searched through drawers and cabinets looking for a lighter or some matches. When she searched in the cabinet, above the stove she found the grill lighter and ran back upstairs to her room. She sat on her bed, lit the Black, and started to smoke. Shakia coughed the first couple of times, but she kept smoking. The room was filled with the stench of Black and Mild.

"Shakia," her mom called from the door. Shakia scrambled around her room. She put the Black out and threw it out of the window. "Hold on, ma." She sprayed perfume trying to get rid of the smell. Her mom walked in the room and looked around. "What were you doing in here?" her mom asked. Shakia continued to fix up her room while her mom was standing in the door way. "Hello, can you hear me talking to you?" her mom announced with an attitude. Shakia looked up and saw her mom scowling at her. "Sorry, I thought you were still standin' at the door."

"What were you doing in here?"

"I was cleanin' up before I go to Sidney's house."

"What's that smell?" Her mom began to look around the room with curiosity. "I don't smell anything." Shakia shrieked nervously. She watched her mom's eyes search her room. "Are you sure you don't want to talk to me about something?" Shakia shook her head scarcely. "I'm about to leave so have fun at Sidney's and tell her mom I said Hi."

She slowly walked out of the room still looking around as she left. Shakia flopped on her bed in relief. She turned to look at the clock; it was seven thirty. As she lay on the bed she heard the front door shut and the car engine start. A few minutes later she went downstairs and began to search the kitchen. She

27

opened the refrigerator and scanned the shelves up and down until she saw a bottle of Crystal on the bottom shelf in the back. She grabbed the bottle of wine and put it on the kitchen counter. The wine had already been opened so she got a plastic cup and poured the wine into the cup. She sat down on the couch and began to drink the wine. As she was waiting for Jalissa, she started to wonder about Sidney and how she had lied to her. Before she knew it, she had drunk the whole cup of Crystal. It started to get warm so she took off her shirt. She looked at the clock and it was 7:50 pm. The only thing she could think about was going to party and looking cute. While she was still waiting for Jalissa she went back to the kitchen to get some more Crystal.

"Ding."

She walked to the front door and looked out of the peep whole. It was Jalissa. She opened the front door and Jalissa pushed her way in. "Nice crib! What do ya people do?" Shakia closed the door and walked back to the kitchen. "My dad's a pastor and my mom sells houses."

While Jalissa looked around the house Shakia poured more Cristal in the cup and sat back on the couch. "You a pastor's kid? Those are the worst ones." Shakia looked at Jalissa with a questioning look. "Are you ready to go?" Jalissa asked. "Yeah." Shakia put on her shirt, grabbed her bag, and headed for the door.

"Kia, you been drinkin' a lil bit?" She turned to look at Jalissa. "Does it look like I was drinkin'?"

"I'm just askin' 'cause you left the bottle on the counter like a genius." They both laughed and Shakia went to put the bottle back in the refrigerator. After she put the wine away, they walked out of the door. They walked towards the car and got in. Jalissa sped off like she was in a rush.

"Where is Ashley and Mercedes?"

"After we get dressed we'll pick them up around ten thirty."

28

As they were driving, Shakia noticed that she was going into a more urban area. She was staring out of the car window in curiosity.

"You ever been on this side of town?"

"No, my mom tries to keep me from this area." Jalissa pulled into her apartment complex and there were boys hanging around the door with pit bulls.

"I hope you not scared of dogs." Shakia shook her head no as Jalissa pulled into the parking space. They got out of the car and Shakia got her bag out of the back. Jalissa waited for her to get her things and they walked towards the building. As they were walking, the boys stopped what they were doing and stared at them until they were in the building.

"Who are they?"

"They live here. They just hustlin'."

Jalissa and Shakia walked up to the third floor. Jalissa walked to her door and said, "It might be a lil loud in here." She opened the door slowly and walked in. When Shakia stepped in there was nothing but chaos. There were three other kids running through the house. The house looked like it had not been cleaned in years, food still on the stove, bottles everywhere, and stains on the wall. Jalissa led Shakia to her room. When she walked in Jalissa's room, she saw it was a little neater than the rest of the house. "Just put ya stuff anywhere." Shakia dropped her things in a corner by the bed. "Where's your mom?"

Jalissa walked in her closet and turned on the light. "She should be comin' home soon, but then she leaves again." Shakia was looking around the room with curiosity.

"We're goin' to leave here at ten or ten fifteen." said Jalissa

"Aight, whose party, is it?"

"We goin' clubbin' tonight." Shakia's eyes grew big at what Jalissa said. "I'm not old enough to get in a club."

"Don't worry 'bout that. I got my connections, you'll be straight." Jalissa continued to search her closet for an outfit. When she finally found what she was looking for it was nine forty. "You need to be gettin' ready."

Shakia got her bag and sat on the bed. She began to take her clothes out of the bag and lay them on the bed. "Where is the bathroom?" Jalissa pointed out of the door and said, "Down the hall and the first door on your left."

She walked to the bathroom and one of Jalissa's little brothers was standing in the bathroom doorway.

"Are you one of Jalissa's friends?"

"Yeah."

He stood in the doorway and stared at her for a while and then he ran off giggling. She didn't pay him any mind and walked in the bathroom. She began to get dressed and she heard the front door slam. Then a woman yelled angrily, "Jalissa! Get out here now!"

"What? I'm gettin' ready to go out."

"No, I'm goin' out. You're stayin' here 'cause you have to watch ya lil brothers."

"Ma, I told you last night I was goin' out."

"Well, you need to cancel ya plans 'cause I'm goin' to the Grown and Sexy with Mick."

Shakia looked both ways before walking out of the bathroom.

"Who the hell are you?" Jalissa's mom exclaimed.

"She's with me," Jalissa said from her room.

Shakia walked back to the room and put her other clothes back into her bag. Jalissa's mom stood in the doorway and stared at Jalissa. "I told you, you not goin' anywhere 'cause I'm goin' out."

"Whatever, that's what you think," Jalissa mumbled to herself. Her mom stormed in the room and slapped Jalissa in the mouth. Jalissa stared at her mom with anger in her eyes; she began to ball her hands into a fist.

"What, you want to hit me?"

Jalissa lay on the bed and stared at the ceiling. Her mom walked down the hallway and then out of the front door. Shakia stood in the corner in shock at what had just happened. Jalissa sat up in the bed and called the oldest of her little brothers. He walked into the room with headphones on. Jalissa took them off and asked, "Can you do me a favor and keep everything straight tonight?"

He stared at her with a disappointed look. "Ok, but why do you and mom always have to leave?"

"I'll be back later on tonight I promise. I'll get you some Jordan's if you do this." Jalissa gave him some money for pizza. He walked out of the room and went back to his room.

~ ~ ~ ~ ~ ~ ~ ~

"Hello," Quincy answered the phone.

"Hey, are you comin' out with us to the Apple Bottom?" Deon'te asked.

"I guess I'll come. I got some homework to finish first."

"Man bump that work. It's gonna be shorties everywhere."

Quincy thought to himself for a second and replied, "Aight I'll be there." He hung up the phone and walked to the kitchen in his house. His dad sat on the couch with a forty-ounce beer in his hand watching TV. Quincy opened the refrigerator looking for something to eat. "You need to get a job and help buy some food in this house," his dad exclaimed from the couch. Quincy ignored his dad and continued to search the refrigerator. "I'm talkin' to you boy."

Quincy slowly closed the refrigerator door and walked into the living room. "You know you act like you deaf sometimes," his dad fussed sarcastically. Quincy sat on the couch across from his dad. "Now, I was sayin' why don't you have a job, you a senior?"

"Well, basketball is gonna get me to the NBA and that takes up all my time." His dad took a sip of the forty ounce and chuckled. "You think you can be in the NBA. Boy you not gonna make it anywhere." Quincy stood up and started to walk to his room.

"Hey sweetie," his mom said walking through the front door. "Hi ma." He grabbed the groceries in her arms, and set them on the kitchen counter. His mom walked up behind him and rubbed his head. "How was your day?" she asked.

"It was ok, until I got home."

"Why, what happened when you got home?"

"Ya husband, he never has anything good to say to me." "Don't worry about him; you know he's been like that ever since he got in that accident." Quincy started to walk back to his room. "Mom can I go out with some friends tonight?"

"What friends?"

He walked back to the kitchen doorway. "Deon'te and some other boys."

"You know I don't like you talking to that boy. He's nothing but trouble."

"I'll be fine, just trust me."

"Ok, what time are you leaving?"

He shrugged his shoulders and walked to his room. As he was walking his dad called him into the living room. "So you have time to go out with your friends, but you can't get a job."

"Leave him alone, let him have fun. You never have anything positive to say to him."

"Was I talkin' to you, woman?"

Quincy turned, and walked to his room, and slammed the door. He laid on his bed and listened to his dad curse and threaten his mom. After they finished arguing, he rummaged through his closet for an outfit. After he found the clothes he got dressed and sat on his bed.

"Ring."

"Hello," he answered.

"Hey, this is Ricky. What you doin tonight?"

"I'm goin' to the Apple Bottom. What you doin'?"

"I was gonna chill at the house and probably go to the movies later."

"Well, how 'bout you come out with me tonight."

"Naw, I'm straight. I'm just goin' to chill at the house."

"Well, I'll holla at you later." Quincy hung up the phone and walked out of his room.

"Ma I'm 'bout to go."

"Ok, honey, have fun and be safe."

He walked out of the front door and got into his car. He sat in his car and began to wonder about Ricky. He started his car, backed out of the driveway, and sped off. As he was driving, he picked up his cell phone and called Ricky.

"Hello, this is Quincy."

"Yeah, what's up?"

"Is it cool if I come over for a sec."

"Yeah, that's fine. Just walk in when you get here." Quincy hung the phone and headed towards Ricky's house. His cell phone rang again. "Hello."

"Yo, where you at?" Deon'te asked.

"I'm on my way. I just have to make a quick stop."

He hung up the phone and pulled into Ricky's driveway. Ricky was standing outside when Quincy got out of the car. "So what's up? I thought you were goin' to the Apple Bottom."

"I want you to roll with me."

Ricky stared at Quincy with a disappointed look on his face. He walked into his house and left the door open waiting for

Quincy to come in. He walked into the house and sat on the couch in the living room.

"Why didn't you tell me you wanted me to go when you called?"

"I don't know."

Ricky walked to his dresser and searched his drawers for some jeans. Quincy walked into his room and sat on the bed. "I didn't want to go without you 'cause you always have my back." "Well, since I'm comin' with you, you have to come with me to one of my Bible studies." Quincy laid on the bed and thought for a moment. "Fine, I choose which day I will go." Ricky put on his jeans and grabbed a shirt while they hurried out of the front door. They got in Quincy's car and drove off.

He turned to Quincy and warned, "You need to be careful about what kind of girls you talk to. I don't want you to mess up ya future because of a one night stand."

"Here we go again. I told you I'm not gonna get caught up." "Aight, I don't want you tellin' me you got some chick pregnant, have some kind of STD, or somethin' like that." Quincy pulled into a parking space at the Apple Bottom, turned off the car, and leaned back in his seat. Ricky opened the door and stepped out. He looked around outside while Quincy was still sitting in the car. He started to walk towards the club, and saw Deon'te standing outside. Quincy got out of the car and stood beside him on the curb.

"Why didn't you tell me he was goin' to be here?" Ricky asked. Quincy looked up, and saw Deon'te waiting by the door. "Oh, I didn't think you would care." They stood on the curb for a while watching cars pass. "So are you goin' to go in or just stand here?" Quincy asked. They walked across the street towards the club. "What's up, Quincy? The shorties lookin' bum tonight." Deon'te said.

The boys walked to the entrance and the guard asked for their I.D. They pulled them out and walked into the club. As

34

they were walking in, Deon'te tried to walk quickly pushing Quincy in front of him. Ricky was struggling to keep up with them. Quincy stopped walking and turned to see if Ricky was still behind them. Ricky was lost in the crowd; he went to sit at the bar. "Where did Ricky go? He was just behind us," Quincy asked. The music was so loud that Deon'te couldn't even hear what he was saying. "Man you better get with one of these females," said Deon'te.

All of a sudden, a girl walked up to Quincy and pulled him onto the dance floor. She led him into the middle of the floor where there was a crowd of people. She began to dance around him. Quincy tried to ignore her and looked around to see if he saw Ricky standing around. The girl started to dance more seductively craving his attention. When he noticed how she was dancing on him, he started to think less about Ricky and more about the girl. After a few minutes passed, Quincy stopped thinking about Ricky and focused more on the girl who was dancing on him. Meanwhile Ricky was sitting at the bar thinking to himself. He left the bar and started to walk around. He saw Deon'te with a couple of girls and a drink in his hand. Ricky saw the bathroom sign and started towards it until he saw Quincy grinding with a girl. He turned his head and Deon'te was staring at him. Ricky walked into the bathroom and stared in the mirror. He lowered his head, and someone walked in the bathroom. He looked up and Deon'te was standing behind him with a sneaky grin.

~ ~ ~ ~ ~ ~ ~ ~ ~

"So, Kia, what did ya mom say 'bout ya new clothes?" Ashley asked. "Why would I even walk around my house with these kinds of clothes on? My mom would never buy me a shirt that shows part of my chest or jeans that are cut so low that they show my thong." Shakia replied. Mercedes and Ashley glanced at each other. "Ya people are some kind of strict. What do they do?"

35

Mercedes asked. Shakia glanced at Jalissa with worry. "My dad is a pastor and my mom sells houses."

Mercedes and Ashley burst into laughter. Shakia turned around and looked at them. "What's so funny 'bout that?"

"We have a Pastor's daughter on our hands. Those are the worst ones," Mercedes exclaimed. "That's the same thing I said," Jalissa replied from the driver's seat. Shakia looked confused. "What you mean the worst ones?" Shakia asked angrily. "Pastor's kids are the badest. They do everything they're not supposed to. Pastor's kids are straight up freaks," Mercedes concluded.

"Who told you that?" Shakia asked.

"What do you mean who told me, look at you. Why do you think you've been sneakin' out of the house and stealin' clothes? We sure didn't make you do it."

Shakia leaned back in the front seat. Jalissa drove around the club and parked in the back alley. The girls stepped out of the car and followed Jalissa to the back door of the club. "What this club called?" Shakia asked.

"This the Apple Bottom" Jalissa answered. She pulled out her cell phone and knocked on the door. "Come to the back door," she told the person on the other end of the phone. The girls waited at the door for maybe a minute. A tall light-skinned man opened the door.

"Hey, girl, long time no see, give me some love," he said. Jalissa greeted him with a big hug and kiss on the cheek. The man stepped back and looked at Ashley and Mercedes. "You brought the two trouble makers with you." He greeted them with a two-cent hug. He looked over their shoulder and saw Shakia standing by a pole. "And who is this sexy dime piece right here?" Shakia walked towards the door and he stopped her in her tracks.

"How you doin' ma?"

"I'm straight and you?"

He looked her up and down, then front to back. Shakia was flattered and began to blush while he was looking at her. "My name is Mario." Shakia shook his hand and replied, "I'm Shakia."

Meanwhile Jalissa, Mercedes, and Ashley were standing at the door waiting for Mario to walk them in. "Could you hurry up," Jalissa rushed him.

Mario grabbed Shakia by the hand and motioned for the girls to go in. They walked through doors and down hallways. Mario was still holding on to Shakia's hand as he was leading them to the main room.

"Shakia, if we get separated here is my cell number or find Mario." Jalissa exclaimed.

It felt like they were walking forever until he stopped. He opened the door; there were seizure lights, smoke, and loud music. They walked in and Jalissa, Mercedes, and Ashley ran onto the dance floor leaving Shakia with Mario. She tried to catch up with them, but Mario pulled her back. "I want to get to know you a lil bit," Mario hinted. Shakia looked into his attractive hazel eyes and replied "Ok."

He led her to a booth next to the bar. As she was walking behind him she noticed men were staring and pointing as she walked by. When they got to the booth she sat down and slid next to the wall. "I'm goin' to get us some drinks." Shakia watched him walk to the bar and order the drinks. While Mario was getting drinks, a man came and sat in the booth with Shakia.

"Can I get ya number?" he asked. Shakia looked at him, then over at Mario. "You don't even know my name."

"If you give me ya number... I'll ask you ya name and whatever else you want me to ask."

Shakia looked up and Mario was standing at the booth. "Excuse me man, that's my girl you tryin' to holla at." The man looked at Mario and then walked off. Mario watched him walk away and placed the drinks on the table and sat next to her.

37

"So how old are you?" he asked.

"Not old enough to be in this club," she answered.

"That didn't answer my question."

"I'm fifteen."

"With a body like that it's hard for me to believe that."

Shakia blushed and turned around looking for Jalissa. While she looked around, Mario slipped a crushed ecstasy pill in her drink. Shakia turned back towards Mario. "So how old are you?" she asked.

"Don't worry 'bout that. Age ain't nothin' but a number." He smiled at her and took a sip of his drink. After she saw Mario sip his drink, she stared at hers for a moment and cocked her head back and took the liquor to the head. Mario gazed at her and grabbed her by the hand, "Let's go dance."

She was hesitant and she finally gave in. He led her to the dance floor. While they were walking through the crowd of people all of a sudden she became light headed and dizzy. She stopped walking and put her hands on her forehead. "I don't feel too good," she exclaimed.

"Do you want to go somewhere more quiet?" he asked. She leaned against him trying to gain her balance.

"Shakia, are you ok?"

She looked at him as if she were high, "I'm fine."

"So you want to get out of here and go to the back."

He grabbed her by the hand and gently pulled her off the dance floor. Mario put his hands on her waist and guided her to a door that read private room.

"Where we goin'?" she asked.

They walked through the door and it looked like a work office. Mario noticed there was a couch in the corner. He struggled trying to keep Shakia on her feet. After walking to the couch, he slowly placed her on the chair. Shakia tried to sit up in the chair, but the ecstasy in her system didn't allow her. Mario walked to the door and looking both ways, slowly shut the door as he turned to walk back into the room. Shakia finally found it in herself to sit up in the chair.

"Take me back to Jalissa," she demanded.

"You're ok. I brought you back here 'cause you looked a lil sick." He walked towards her and stood directly in front of her. She looked up at him. "Where are we?" "You're fine. I just wanted to get you away from all those people."

He sat next to her with his arm around her shoulder. Closer and closer he moved towards her, while she struggled to stay awake. When she noticed he was moving closer to her, she stood up as quickly as she could and started for the door. Mario ran in front of her so she could not walk out of the door. "Move! I want to go back to Jalissa," she whined slowly trying to keep herself balanced. "I just want to make sure you're ok 'cause you look sick," he replied as he grabbed her by the arms.

"No, take me to Jalissa."

"Just sit down and I'll take care of you."

Mario grabbed her wrist and tried to pull her to the couch. Shakia jerked away, flying backwards falling onto the floor. She laid on the floor and then started scooting across it trying to keep away from him. He slowly walked towards her trying not to scare her.

"Why do I feel like this?"

"I'm tryin' to help you if you let me," he said helping her off the floor, then sitting her on the couch.

Shakia laid down on the couch closing her eyes because the room would not stop spinning and everything was dizzy. While she was lying on the couch Mario was staring at her with lust in his eyes. He sat on the edge the of couch, stroking his fingers through her hair, trying to relax her. Shakia slowly opened her eyes with tears rolling down her cheeks. "What's wrong with me?" Mario placed his hand on her stomach, "Just relax. You're just scared."

Shakia began to take deep breaths trying to relax. Mario slowly moved his hand down her stomach unbuttoning her pants. Shakia quickly sat up on the couch and scooted away from him. "What you doin'?" she asked. Mario didn't answer; he just moved closer to Shakia. She stood up and headed for the door. Mario ran in front of her and stepped in front of the door.

"I don't think you should go anywhere 'cause you drank too much." He gripped her wrist and forced himself on her. "Stop! Let me go!" Shakia fought to break free, but the more she fought the tighter his grip became. "Help!" Mario pushed her on the floor and forced himself on top of her. "Help!" she screamed hoping someone would hear her crying out.

Mario put his hand over her mouth to stop her from screaming. He unbuttoned his pants with his hand still over her mouth. Shakia was screaming to the top of her lungs, while trying to get away. He pulled her pants with one hand and the other still over her mouth.

"Please let me go!" she yelled. All of a sudden she felt a sharp pain going in and out of her body. Tears were balling down her face. "Stop! Please Stop!" she cried with his hand still over her mouth.

Mario ignored her cries and continued to have his way with her. As she was laying there helplessly, all she could think about was the pain he was putting her through. Shakia continued to scream hoping and praying someone would hear her.

"Help! Somebody please!"

<u>Comfort - 2 Corinthians 1:3,4</u> - *Blessed be the God and Father of our Lord Jesus Christ, the Father of mercies and God of all comfort, who comforts us in all our tribulation, that we may be able to comfort those who are in any trouble, with the comfort with which we ourselves are comforted by God.*

~ Chapter Four~

TRAPPED...

TRAPPED

Ricky jumped in shock when he looked up and saw Deon'te in the reflection of the mirror. "You scared the mess out of me," Ricky cried as he put his head back down on the sink. Deon'te leaned on the bathroom door waiting for Ricky to face him. "What's the problem?" Ricky turned to him and asked. "Why you always blockin' Quincy from doin' what he want to do?" asked Deon'te. Ricky looked at him with suspense, "What you mean blockin'? I'm tryin' to help my boy focus on life." Deon'te walked toward Ricky rubbing his hand as if he were going to hit him. "You know what... it's niggas like you that get on my last nerve. You think life is all about sex, drugs, and money!" Ricky exclaimed. Deon'te stepped in Ricky's face with fire in his eyes. "I think you need to watch who you talkin' to, 'cause you have no clue of who you dealin' with," Deon'te told Ricky, while lifting his shirt to show his pistol. Ricky backed away showing no fear. "A piece of steel don't faze me." he said. "Well all I'm goin' to tell you is stay out my way, don't be no fool cause if you mess with fire you will get burned." Deon'te swung the bathroom door open and walked out.

Ricky looked in the mirror taking a deep breath, "God help me." Suddenly Quincy walked in the bathroom, "I've been lookin' for you." Ricky looked at Quincy angrily trying not to go off. "Oh, ok you were lookin' for me alright. I don't call grindin' on some girl really lookin'," he replied sarcastically.

"My bad yo, I thought you were right behind me. On my nigga's I'm not lyin', I was lookin' for you until this girl started dancin' on me," Ricky stepped away from the mirrors and leaned against the wall.

"You should leave Deon'te alone 'cause old dude is bad news I'm tellin' you," Quincy rolled his eyes, with an annoyed look on his face.

"Why are you worried about him? Just let him do what he do," Quincy stated.

"You think you know him. I know some stuff about him that will make you think twice about being cool with him." Ricky looked at him in the eyes with care and concern.

"Well, I'm 'bout to chill in here for a sec. You goin' to go back to the party?" Quincy asked.

"Naw I'm goin' to go for a walk and see what restaurants are open at one thirty. Call me when you are ready to go. I won't be far," Ricky exclaimed as he walked out of the bathroom. As Ricky was walking out, Deon'te was coming in.

"Yo, why you in here? The party is out there."

"Naw man," Quincy replied, "I'm just goin' to chill in here for a sec," Deon'te opened the door and two light skinned girls with long black hair walked in.

"If you not gonna come to the party, I'll bring the party to you." Quincy sat in a chair in the corner and the two girls sat on his lap. He put his arms around their waist, "So what's your name?" he asked the girl on his right leg.

"Shante."

"And what's yours?" he asked the other.

"Courtni."

Deon'te was guarding the door making sure nobody came in.

"Let's go outside," Deon'te suggested. They all walked out of the bathroom; the girls clinging to Quincy's arms. When they got outside, Deon'te led them to the alley behind the club. When they stopped, two dumpsters and a brick wall showed the end of the alley. Deon'te reached in his pocket, pulled out a cigar, lighter, blade, and a sandwich bag half full of weed. With the girls still clinging to his arms, Quincy walked over to Deon'te to see what he was doing. Deon'te walked over to the dumpster, and placed everything on the top if it.

"What you doin'?" Quincy asked.

"We 'bout to light up," Deon'te answered. The girls let go of his arms, walked over to Deon'te, and began to smile. "Naw, man I can't do that," Quincy said. Deont'te rolled the blunt and then let the girls smell it.

"That's some good stuff," Shante shrieked. She grabbed the lighter off the dumpster, lit the blunt, and took a puff. She held the smoke in for a moment and then let it out of her nose. "I ain't puffed in a good minute," she exclaimed. She passed it to Courtni and she inhaled deeply, then blew the smoke in Quincy's face. After she took another puff, she passed it to Deon'te.

"Now let me show ya'll how a pro get down," he chuckled. The girls began to giggle as Deon'te inhaled. He handed the blunt to Quincy, expecting him to take it. Quincy took a step back shaking his head, no.

"Stop bein' a punk and hit this before we smoke it all," Deon'te said. "Come on baby it won't mess you up. It will just make you feel a lil goofy," Shante explained putting the blunt to his lips.

Quincy parted his lips and began to inhale. He coughed as smoke came out of his mouth. He tried to pass it but Deon'te pushed his hand back towards him. He looked at the girls and took another puff.

~ ~ ~ ~ ~ ~ ~ ~ ~

Mario slowly got up leaving Shakia lying on the floor with blood in between her legs. He buttoned his pants and stood by the door watching her tremble with fear and pain.

"If you tell anybody, even Jalissa, 'bout this I swear I'll find you and you don't want me to do that," he threatened as he was walking out of the door.

Shakia slowly sat up looking between her legs staring at the blood. Tears ran down her face as she picked herself up off the floor. Then she looked around the room finding a blanket lying across the arm of the couch. She limped over to the couch and slowly sat down trying not to put too much pain on herself. With tears running down her cheeks, she grabbed the blanket and cleaned the blood from between her legs. After she was done, she stuffed the blanket behind the couch so no one would see it. Shakia continued to cry in the fetal position on the couch rocking back and forth trying to comfort herself. While she was rocking, she thought of her mom, and how she had disobeyed and let her down. Soon she found enough strength to get herself together, fixing her hair and cleaning her clothes off. As she stood up, she could feel nothing but pain as she tried to walk. Shakia walked around the room trying to work out the pain. When she finally found enough strength to leave the room, she turned to get another look at the room where she was raped and she walked out.

People were still drinking and dancing. Mario was staring at her from the bar making sure she didn't make a scene. Shakia started to walk around the club as if she didn't know where she was. The lights flashing, the loud music, and the ecstasy still in her system made her feel as if she were going to pass out. She stumbled trying to keep her balance until she saw a chair by the wall. As she was making her way to the chair, a man came from behind a corner. After him came Jalissa counting money and stuffing it in her bra.

She looked at Shakia, "Hey where you been. I saw you walk out with Mario. What ya'll do?" Shakia just sat in the chair staring at the ground, ignoring Jalissa.

"Oh, you actin' like you can't hear me. Did old dude turn you out so good that you can't talk." Shakia looked up slowly and focused her eyes on Jalissa. Mario quickly got up pushing his way through the crowd. He walked over to Jalissa and put his arm around her waist. "So where you been all night?" he asked. He glanced over at Shakia in innocence with his hazel eyes.

"I been dancin' and makin' some money, if you know what I mean," Jalissa bragged as she wiped the corners of her mouth. Shakia just sat in the chair staring at the floor as if she were scared to talk.

"What's wrong with you?" Jalissa asked Shakia.
Mario glared at her making sure she didn't say anything.

"Nothing I'm just a lil tired," Shakia answered in fear.

"Well, I'm about to holla at some ladies. I'll talk to ya'll later. Oh, and nice to meet you, Shakia," he said. He winked at her and walked off. Jalissa watched him walk away.

"Did ya'll do the grown up or somthin'?"
Shakia looked at Jalissa trying not to cry.

"Was he ya first? If he was, I know you are in some pain, 'cause he is a grown man," Jalissa said playfully.
Shakia nodded her head yes, as if she were ashamed.

"Congrats, you must be some kind of good 'cause I haven't even done it with his sexy tail." Jalissa leaned against the wall dancing to the music. "When we leavin'?" Shakia asked.

"I don't know, but it's only two o'clock." All of a sudden Jalissa grabbed Shakia by the wrist and ran on the dance floor. When they stopped, Jalissa started to dance with Shakia. "Why you bring me out here? I said I was tired." Shakia whined.

"Have a lil fun. You need to get that goody girl out. You only live life once." answered Jalissa

Jalissa continued to dance with her until some random man came up behind Jalissa. Shakia looked around at everybody else having a good time. Jalissa slightly pushed the man she was dancing with behind Shakia. He grabbed her hands and started grinding on her. She was too sore to move but she found a little energy in herself to dance with him. Jalissa stepped back and watched Shakia with a smile. She turned around and found herself another partner. While Shakia was dancing on the man, he let go of her hands and placed his on her thighs. She didn't even notice what he did until he started to move his hands up and down her thighs as she was dancing. When he did that, the image of Mario popped into her head. She stopped dancing and started to walk off. He grabbed her hand trying to stop her.

"Where you goin' ma?" Shakia looked at him and walked off. Jalissa saw her walking off and ran after her.

When she caught up with her, Jalissa stepped in front of her, "Why you leave? He was gettin' into you!"

"He started gettin' too feely."

"Girl, what you mean too feely? When he's not touchin' you that's when you should worry." Shakia looked at the clock, and then at Jalissa.

"Come on, let's go back out there," Jalissa suggested, tugging on Shakia's arm. Just when they were about to go back on the floor Jalissa's phone rang. "Hello," she answered.

"Hey this Ashley. We need to go 'cause Mercedes is piss drunk and she 'bout to fight some chick."

"Where are ya'll?" Jalissa asked.

"We're outside; I'm tryin' to calm her down."

"Aight I'm comin'." Jalissa hung up the phone and headed towards the door.

"What happened?" Shakia asked.

"Mercedes is drunk and started some mess, so we about to leave." Shakia took a deep breath in relief. She followed Jalissa outside. She saw Mario kissing a woman in the corner by the bar. When they got outside, Mercedes was walking up and down the street cussing at anything or anybody that moved.

Jalissa went and stood by Ashley, "I thought you were tryin' to calm her down!" Jalissa exclaimed.

"I tried but she was gettin' crazy. She was swingin' and cussin' me out so I let her go." Shakia leaned on the outside of the club waiting for Jalissa to get her under control. Mercedes started walking back towards the club cussing at Jalissa.

"Where the hell you been? Me and Ashley needed you 'cause these girls tried to bank me. And you was in there with that church hoe." Mercedes stepped in Jalissa's face with alcohol on her breath. Jalissa just stared at her making a fool of herself.

"Chick, don't come at me like that. You need to get ya drunk self in the car. And don't ever in ya life come at me like that again."

She headed toward the car trying to walk straight and noticed Shakia leaning on the wall. "What the hell you lookin' at?" she shrieked, walking past Shakia.

Jalissa walked over and stood by Shakia, "Don't let her get to you; she just hatin' 'cause all the attention not on her."

Ashley walked across the street to help Mercedes find the car. Jalissa put her arm around Shakia's shoulder and they walked towards the car. When they were all settled in the car, Jalissa pulled out of the parking lot and drove off.

"Kia, what you think 'bout Mario?"

"He's sexy as hell." Ashley exclaimed from the back seat. Shakia thought to herself for a moment then said, "Yeah, he's aight. Why ya'll keep askin' me 'bout him?" Jalissa turned around and smiled at Ashley.

"'Cause he was lookin' at you like he wanted you." Ashley added.

"I think he did you a favor and popped that cherry," Jalissa added. Mercedes burst into laughter, "You nothin' but a scank hoe tryin' to act like an innocent church girl."

Shakia looked out of the window trying her best to ignore the comment.

"Stop hatin' on the girl. You just mad. She got some from Mario and you didn't," Jalissa exclaimed.

Mercedes leaned forward towards Shakia, "I'm not like Jalissa, I don't like you, so you best stay out my way," She whispered in her ear.

Shakia leaned forward in the seat and looked at Jalissa.

"What else we doin' tonight?" she asked.

"I got somthin' planned, after we take the drunky and Ashley home." As Jalissa and Shakia were talking, Mercedes opened the door and threw up while the car was still moving. Jalissa slammed on the brakes, and let Mercedes get it all out of her system.

"You lucky nobody was behind me. Now you goin' to think twice about drinkin' so much," Jalisa told her while she was still throwing up. Mercedes shut the car door and slouched in the seat.

"Are we at my house yet?" she asked.

"Yeah, we almost there," Ashley answered.

Shakia leaned over to Jalissa, "Why she always messin' with me?"

"She's just jealous 'cause you gettin' stuff she wanted." Jalissa stopped the car in front of a house that looked like it had been through World War II.

"Hey you alcoholic, you're home." Mercedes slowly opened the car door and fell out.

"Yo, I'm goin' to stay with her tonight and make sure she don't do nothin crazy," Ashley replied.

"Aight yo I'll call you tomorrow." Ashley got out of the car and walked over to help Mercedes off the ground; while Ashley helped her up Mercedes mugged Shakia and flicked her off as she walked in the house.

"That's the kind of stuff I'm talkin' 'bout," Shakia exclaimed.

"Don't worry 'bout her. I got you," Jalissa replied putting her hand on Shakia's leg. Jalissa winked at her with a smile and removed her hand from her leg and drove off. Shakia looked out of the window remembering what Mario did to her. Tears began to fall from her eyes.

"I hope you not cryin' because of Mercedes." Shakia wiped her eyes and looked at Jalissa with a two-cent smile.

"I'm fine. I just got some stuff on my mind."

"Oh, well I got some stuff that will take ya mind off of everything."

"I already had a drink and that made me feel funny," Shakia replied. Jalissa pulled into her apartment complex. "I don't know what you had but this stuff I'm 'bout to get will calm you down."

Shakia looked out of the window and noticed that the same boys were still standing at the entrance of Jalissa's apartment. Jalissa parked the car, got out, and walked over to the boys. Shakia got out slowly after her, as Jalissa conversed with them. She walked up beside Jalissa waiting for her to go into the building. "Go on up and I'll be there in a sec," Jalissa told her. Shakia walked halfway up the steps and turned back to see what Jalissa was doing. While Shakia was looking, Jalissa handed the boy some money and he handed her a bag filled with weed.

"Hey, Jalissa, put me down with ya girl, she got body," the boy said. Jalissa looked at him and then ran up the stairs making sure Shakia could not hear her.

"Nigga please, you know what's up," she replied.

"Oh, so it's like that? Can I come up to?" he asked. Jalissa looked at him and laughed.

"Boy please, you got me mixed up." Jalissa put the weed in her pocket, and started up the steps. When she was halfway up the stairs she saw Shakia looking over the rail.

"What you doin'? I thought I told you to go up the stairs." They walked up to Jalissa's apartment and stopped.

"What you get from 'em?"

"Don't worry 'bout that, just know that yo problems will go away for tonight." Jalissa opened the door and let Shakia in first. She turned on the light and the house still looked a mess.

"Go to my room and I'll be in there in a minute." Shakia walked into Jalissa's room and changed into a tank top and shorts. While Shakia was changing, Jalissa was in the kitchen getting two beers out of the refrigerator. After leaving the kitchen, she checked her brothers' and sisters' rooms to see if they were asleep. She walked in her room as Shakia was putting on her shorts.

Jalissa bit her bottom lip, "I know you not ready to go to sleep." She took the weed out of her pocket and placed it on the dresser.

"What's in the bag?" Shakia asked. Jalissa took a Black and split it open with a razor. Shakia sat on the bed waiting for Jalissa as she took the tobacco out of the black. Then she put the weed in the open black and rolled it up. She held it up in front of Shakia knowing she would take it. Shakia took the blunt and examined it before she smoked it.

"It's not goin' to hurt. It's just goin' to make you feel better. Whatever's botherin' you must really be important 'cause you were cryin'." Shakia looked at Jalissa and put the blunt to her lips and inhaled.

"Now, hold it in for a sec." She blew out the smoke, and then coughed continuously. As she tried to hand the blunt back to Jalissa, Jalissa stared at her waiting for her to inhale it again.

"Why you givin' it to me? Keep smokin' 'cause you don't have the full effect yet." She took another puff of the blunt and held it in for about five seconds before letting it out. Jalissa sat on the edge of the bed waiting for the drug to get in her system. A couple minutes later Shakia burst into laughter uncontrollably. When Jalissa noticed the drug was working she started to scoot closer to her looking her up and down.

"You know what I want to do?" Shakia asked playfully. Jalissa just looked at her as if she were waiting to make a move.

"What you want to do?" Shakia put her legs on Jalissa and laid back on the bed.

"Whatever you want to do!" Shakia said. She looked at the ceiling. "Jalissa, do you think I'm pretty?" Shakia asked.

Jalissa slowly slid her hand on Shakia's inner thigh, "Yea, you been pullin' niggas left and right. The only thing I suggest you change is ya clothes." Jalissa began to rub her inner thigh. Shakia was so high that she didn't care what Jalissa was doing. She took another puff and blew the smoke in Jalissa's face. Jalissa laid beside her on the bed, as if she wanted to cuddle with her.

"What's the craziest thing you ever did?" Shakia asked taking another puff of the blunt. Jalissa rolled on her back then looked at Shakia with eyes of care. "My craziest thing was probably kissin' a girl." Jalissa answered. Shakia paused for a moment then burst into laughter again. "You one of those girls gone wild."

Jalissa grabbed the blunt, took two puffs and then passed it back. "What's the craziest thing you ever did?" Jalissa asked. Shakia smoked the blunt and thought to herself. "Umm, sneakin' out the house, smokin' a blunt, and havin' sex with a twenty-somethin'- year-old man." They both looked at each other and giggled. Jalissa gazed at Shakia lustfully as she took another puff of the blunt.

"If my mom knew what I was doin I would be on punishment for life," Shakia exclaimed as if she didn't care. Jalissa started to stroke Shakia's neck slowly with her fingers. "Well, what momma don't know won't hurt her." She continued to stroke Shakia's neck with her fingers.

"What you doin'?" Shakia asked playfully. Jalissa sat up on the bed then leaned over her. She started to rub her leg slowly as if she wanted to kiss her.

"Why you touchin' me like that? Do you want me to be a girl gone wild, too?" Shakia continued to let Jalissa rub her legs until suddenly Shakia pulled her down by the neck, then kissed her. After they kissed Shakia laughed.

"I have a crazy side, too," she said taking another puff. Jalissa took the blunt from Shakia and put it in the ash tray. Shakia laid on the bed feeling as high as a kite.

"I can't believe I kissed you."

"Oh, that's cool. That kind of stuff don't bother me," Jalissa replied. "To tell you the truth, I kind of like it," Shakia exclaimed. Jalissa leaned down and kissed her again with no hesitation. As they kissed, Shakia felt Jalissa touching her all over her body, not knowing what would happen next. Jalissa lifted Shakia's shirt trying to take it off. Shakia started to warm up to Jalissa and then rolled on top of her.

~ ~ ~ ~ ~ ~ ~ ~

"How many of these did we smoke?" Quincy asked. Deon'te looked around and then chuckled, "I couldn't tell you, dawg." Quincy leaned forward and looked at the girls sitting beside Deon'te. "Do ya'll know how many we smoked?" he asked them.

Shante leaned forward with a grin on her face, "Sweetie, hell if I know. But I can tell you we high as hell." They all looked at each other and burst into laughter. The two girls continued to laugh even though Quincy and Deon'te stopped.

"Yo you need to get with Courtni 'cause she been buggin' me 'bout you all night," Deon'te suggested as he rolled another blunt. Quincy reached for the blunt, then took two puffs and passed it back. "I don't know man, she ain't said nothin' to me. Plus she looks like she grown."

"That's 'cause she is. They think we twenty-three." Quincy laughed and reached for the blunt again.

"Man, you terrible. If I do anything with that woman we goin' to get some food 'cause I got the munchies." Shante leaned forward to look at Quincy; examining him.

"Yea, just go over there and do what you always do to get a man to get with you." Courtni slowly got up holding onto the wall trying to keep herself from falling. While she was walking, the boys stopped smoking and watched her walk past until she sat down by Quincy. Deon'te scooted toward Shante and passed her the blunt. Meanwhile, Courtni started talking to Quincy. "How old are you again?" Quincy paused for a moment not knowing if he wanted to tell the truth or say he was twenty-three. "Umm, I'm twenty-three." Courtni leaned on his shoulder in a flirtatious way.

"Why you sit by me?" She lifted her head and looked into his eyes as if she were casting a spell on him.

"'Cause I want somethin' from you." She stood up then reaching for his hand helping him up. They walked to the street and headed towards her car. Suddenly Quincy heard his name being called from a distance. He stopped walking and looked around to see where it was coming from.

"What's wrong?" Courtni asked. He looked at her, shook his head, and continued to her car. Then he heard his name again and he looked around towards him. Quincy stopped again trying to figure out who was running at him. When the person got closer he noticed it was Ricky. Courtni tugged on his arm trying to signal him to keep walking. Once Ricky finally caught up with them, he put his hands overhead trying to catch his breath. "Where you been? I was in and out of the club lookin' for you. It's three in the mornin'," Ricky said, still catching his breath.

"I been with Deon'te. We were chillin' behind the club with my new friend Courtni," Quincy replied with a goofy smile on his face. Ricky started to sniff the air, "What's that smell?" Quincy and Courtni started to chuckle as Ricky continued to sniff trying to find the smell. "It smells like reefa out here." He looked at Quincy's eyes and noticed his eyelids were smaller than normal. Quincy just stood there with a sneaky smirk on his face.

"I know you didn't do what I think you did," Ricky exclaimed. Quincy and Courtni looked at each other and burst into laughter. "Who is this dude?" Courtni asked Quincy, still giggling. Quincy ignored the question and continued to look at Ricky with a sneaky smirk. "Come on Q. I thought you had more sense than that." Ricky said.

"It's not like I'm drunk like I was last time and plus I know everything I'm doin'," Quincy replied.

"Oh, really you know what ya doin? Well, what 'bout now?"

"Well, I was goin' to go with my new friend Courtni to her car and chill," Quincy said, putting his arm around her shoulder.

"To tell you the truth, dawg, I thought you had a lil more smarts and self control."

Quincy chuckled to himself, "I'm just enjoyin' my years while I'm young and sexy." Courtni tugged on his arm hoping he would budge. When he didn't move, Courtni rolled her eyes at Ricky and walked off.

"Hey girl, where you goin'?" Quincy asked. She stopped and turned, "I can see you got some business to handle so I will be in the car waitin' if you even come.

"You got a problem. You always ask me to come somewhere with you, then you do some crazy stuff, knowin' good and well I'm goin' to have a problem with it." Quincy leaned on the stop sign as if he didn't care what Ricky was saying.

While Ricky continued to talk, Deon'te walked from the alley zipping his pants. When he saw Ricky fussing at Quincy he yelled, "Church boy where you been, you missed the party." Ricky turned around and saw Deon'te casually making his way towards them. He turned back around and faced Quincy.

"Well, I'm ready to go and you need to go home and sleep this stuff off."

"What you mean go home? It's still early," Deon'te complained standing behind Ricky.

"I'm not goin' home yet," Quincy added.

"Boy, you know it's three somethin' in the mornin'." Then Ricky looked at Deon'te and noticed his eyes were just as small as Quincy's.

"Well, you stay out here if you want to, I'm goin' home. Don't ask me to come with you anywhere if you goin' to act like this." Ricky walked off heading home. Quincy watched Ricky walk down the street as if he didn't care. Deon'te walked over to Quincy and shook his head giggling.

"How many times do I got to tell you dawg, you need to drop the church boy." Quincy glanced at him and headed to Deon'te's car. "Where you goin'? I thought you were goin with Courtni," Deon'te said as he followed Quincy to the car. "I was but Ricky saw me walkin' with her to her car." They both laughed until they got in the car. Once they were settled in the car, Deon'te put the key in the ignition then started it.

"I have to make a quick stop before I take you home," Deon'te mentioned as sped off.

"I told you I don't want to go home." While they were driving, Quincy began to think about his dad and how he puts him down. Deon'te turned on the radio as he was driving and he noticed Quincy got quiet. He turned off the radio.

"Yo, what's wrong with you? Why you get so quiet?"

"I need some paper in my pocket. I'm broke and I'm tired of borrowin' money from my mom." Deon'te dug in his pocket and pulled out a wad of money wrapped in a rubber band.

"I can put you down with my type of work if you really need the money," Deonte suggested. Quincy glanced at the money and put his hand on his head.

"Dawg, I'm tellin' you trappin' is the easiest way to get paper." Deon'te reached in his other pocket and pulled out a pack of cigarettes and put the money on the dashboard of the car.

"I don't know 'bout trappin'. It's too risky; that can mess up my scholarship."

"You act like they goin' to find out. Plus do you even have time for a job? Basketball got you tied up. When you trap you can get money anytime of the day."

Quincy leaned his head back and took a deep breath, "Let me think 'bout it for a sec."

"Well, while you thinkin' smoke this," Deon'te suggested as he handed him the cigarette. Quincy lit it and smoked as if he were smoking his whole life. He looked at the wad of money still sitting on the dashboard.

"Aight man, put me down."

"Now that's what's up. I'm goin' to give you some reefa and ex to start out."

Deon'te slowed down and parked in front of a grocery shop. Quincy threw the cigarette out of the window and reclined his seat back. Deon'te took the money off the dashboard and put two hundred dollars in Quincy's hand.

"I don't know 'bout you, but I got the munchies. I'm about to get some food out of here. I'll be right back." Before Deon'te opened the door he tossed a sandwich bag filled with weed and a half-filled bag of ecstasy on his lap.

"If somebody come up to the car askin' for some get that money man." He chuckled as he stepped out of the car. Quincy watched him walk into the store and then stared at the drugs lying on his lap.

"What am I gettin' myself into?" he murmured to himself. While he was waiting for Deon'te to leave the store a man with a black hoodie walked up to his window.

"Hey, man you got some ex?" the man asked paranoid. The man looked around quickly as if he thought someone were following him. Quincy opened the bag of ecstasy and took out four pills. The man threw ten dollars in the car and rushed Quincy to give him the pills. He gave the man his money's worth and quickly rolled up his window. The man counted the pills, looked left, then right, then quickly walked off. Deon'te stepped out of the store with a large bag filled with junk food. He walked to the car, opened the door, and handed the groceries to Quincy. After Deon'te sat in the car he took the groceries and placed them in the back seat. "I see you got some action," Deon'te assured with a smile.

"I guess you can say that. He just threw the money in the car and I think he was addicted 'cause he was in a rush to get the ex."

"You need to get yaself organized. I guess you can do that tomorrow," Deon'te sugessted. All of a sudden, a black Benz pulled up behind Deon'te and flashed the headlights twice.

Deon'te looked in the rear view mirror, "Aww, not this man again," he moaned to himself. Deon'te turned around, rumbling through the back seat. When he found what he was looking for he put on a hoodie and put a berretta in the pocket of the hoodie.

"I'll be right back," he told Quincy. He got out of the car and walked to the driver's window, leaning over with his hands in the pocket of the hoodie. Meanwhile Quincy was looking through his mirror trying to see what was going on. He saw Deon'te laugh and figured there would be no problem. He put the ten dollars in his pocket and leaned back in the seat.

"Bang! Bang!" Quincy jumped in his seat and looked around. Suddenly Deon'te hopped in the car and sped off.

"What the hell was that?" Quincy exclaimed.

"What you think? I shot that nigga," Deon'te said as he sped down the lonely street.

"What you do that for?"

"Don't worry 'bout that. You just need to get home. "Where ya house at?"

"It's on the next left." Deon'te sped around the corner as if he were in a race.

"Stop right here." Quincy shouted.

Deon'te slammed on brakes, "Hurry up! I'll call you tomorrow and I'll tell you what's up." Quincy quickly gathered his things and got out of the car. Once he got out he watched Deon'te speed down the street. Quincy walked to his door covering the drugs with his shirt knowing his dad would be waiting for him.

Temptation - 2 Timothy 2:22

Flee also youthful lusts; but pursue righteousness, faith, love, peace with those who call on the Lord out of a pure heart.

~ Chapter Five~

MONTHS LATER...

MONTHS LATER...

"Shakia, Mrs. Cousins will see you now," the counselor's secretary informed. Shakia walked down the hall and turned into Mrs. Cousin's office. "Wow, your outfit is a little bit out of dress code. Come in and have a seat," Mrs. Cousins said while Shakia was standing in the doorway. Shakia walked in the office and plopped on the couch. She slouched down in the couch as if she were at home watching TV.

"Do you know why I called you in here?" Mrs. Cousins asked. "No, not really... probably to waste my time," Shakia replied staring out of the window. Mrs. Cousins took a deep breath trying to figure out why Shakia was being so rude. "Well, your teachers and I have noticed your grades have dropped tremendously. And we want to know what's going on with you."

"Nothin'. School is just getting harder that's all," Shakia muttered with a smirk on her face.

"No, something must be wrong because you can't go from straight A's to C's D's and F's without there being a problem."

"Like I told you it's just gettin' harder."

"And your teachers have notified me that your attendance and participation in class is not an everyday thing. Can you explain to me what that is all about?" Shakia stared at the floor ignoring Mrs. Cousins question. "Shakia can you answer that question for me?" She continued to stare at the floor. "Are we done with this lil counselin' session 'cause I have to be somewhere in a few minutes," Shakia added defiantly.

"No, I have noticed the group of girls you've chosen to hang with. I'm going to let you know now they're not what you need in your life. Those girls could care less about you and themselves."

"Don't worry 'bout who I roll with. That's my choice and what I do ain't got nothin' to do with you, so I think you need to keep ya nose out of my business." Mrs. Cousins was speechless.

"Since you feel that way I'm going to schedule a parent teacher conference. Your mom will be talking with all of your teachers."

"You're tellin' me this why? You act like I care. To tell you the truth I could care less," Shakia replied with an attitude.

"Well since you don't care about anything, go back to class and I will be checking with your teacher and find out if you are in class." Shakia rolled her eyes and stormed out of the office. When she got into the hallway, she saw Sidney coming from the library.

"Hey, Shakia, hold up for a sec," Sidney yelled. Shakia kept walking like she didn't hear Sidney call her. Once Sidney finally caught up with her, Shakia continued to walk.

"Hey, slow down I want to ask you somethin'," Sidney exclaimed. Shakia finally stopped walking and focused her attention on Sidney.

"What's up? How come you don't call or even hang with me or the girls anymore?"

Shakia sighed, then rolled her eyes. "Look at me now. Look at you. We are two different people. We don't have anything in common anymore." Sidney stared at Shakia with tears ready to fall from her eyes.

"We were best friends. What happened?" Sidney asked.

"I just grew out of ya'll," Shakia said as she watched a boy walk by. "Well, I don't think you know this but I have a boyfriend now."

Shakia glanced at her, "Really who is it?"

"You remember a couple of months ago when I saw the boy walkin' down the hallway on the way to lunch. Well, his name is Ricky and we go with each other."

Shakia laughed to herself, "You go with church boy. Wow, I would have never guessed."

"You're the one whose dad is a preacher," Sidney replied. Shakia quickly glanced at her with an angry look.

"Why do you roll with her?" Sidney asked as Jalissa was walking down the hallway.

"Don't worry 'bout her. Just know that she's on my level--somethin' that ya not. I'm 'bout to go. I will see you around. Have fun with ya boyfriend." Shakia teased as she walked off. Sidney stood there and watched her walk towards Jalissa with excitement.

Once Shakia met up with Jalissa, Jalissa pointed to Sidney walking away, "What was up with that?"

"She just wanted to talk."

"Oh… you ready to go 'cause I've had enough school for today." Jalissa exclaimed.

"Yea school is 'bout to be over anyway."

"Ashley and Mercedes didn't come to school so we don't have to wait on them." Jalissa said. They walked towards the gym and then walked through the side doors of the school. Once they got to the car Shakia searched the glove compartment.

"Where the Black's? I need one bad today 'cause my counselor talkin' 'bout callin' a parent teacher conference with all my teachers."

"Dang… so you think ya mom goin' to trip?"

"Hell yea… she don't play when it comes to school. But on the serious note she probably don't have time 'cause ever since she started this job thing she's never at home. Her work and bein' a pastor's wife got her busy; and my dad is so wrapped up in church he's barely at home." As Jalissa was driving, she reached in her purse and pulled out a pack of cigarettes and then tossed them on Shakia's lap. "That's what's up. I need somethin' to smoke right now."

"I got somewhere to go today so I'm takin' you home and if somethin' is goin' down tonight I'll call you." Shakia lit one of the cigarettes. "Well, I need to go home anyway 'cause I want to erase my counselor's message off the answerin' machine."

Jalissa laughed, "Girl... you wild."

"You the one that made me this way." As they pulled into Shakia's driveway she put out the cigarette and threw it out of the window.

"Thanks, girl, I'll holla at you later."

"Hold up chick, I'm thirsty. I'm gettin' somethin' to drink." They walked in the house and Jalissa headed straight for the kitchen. While Jalissa was in the kitchen Shakia was spraying perfume on herself trying to cover up the smell of cigarettes.

"What ya'll got to drink?"

"Nothin' but water, juice, and soda."

"You slakin' on your pimpin'. You don't have a stash of liquor or some kind of alcohol anywhere?"

"Girl please... my mom is like Inspector Gadget. She goes through everything."

"She must not check everything 'cause you have clothes in that closet that will make her put you on lock down for life." All of a sudden they heard the front door shut.

"Shakia... sweetie are you home?" Her mom called. Shakia walked out of the kitchen and met her mom in the front room.

"Why are you home so early?" her mom asked.

"My friend Jalissa brought me home. I didn't want to ride the bus." Jalissa walked in holding a soda in her hand.

"Hi how you doin'? I'm Jalissa."

Shakia's mom looked at Jalissa's clothes and saw that she looked a little older than Shakia. "I'm fine how are you?"

"I'm fine just droppin' ya daughter off." Shakia's mom scanned Jalissa up and down.

"How old are you, Jalissa?"

"I'm seventeen. I will be eighteen in December."

Shakia's mom put her things on the couch and continued to question Jalissa. "What grade are you in?"

"I'm in the twelfth."

"Ma stop quizin' her!"

"That's fine Kia, but I have to go now. Nice to meet you and Shakia I'll call you later." As Jalissa was walking towards the door she turned around and winked at Shakia, then walked out of the door. When Jalissa left, Shakia started to go up the stairs heading for her room.

"You know you're too young to be hanging with her."

"Ma please... I'm not too young. You just don't want me to have a life, that's all."

"Who do you think you're talking to? I'm not Jalissa. Now what I say goes and what are you wearing? That outfit is too revealing for you to be wearing."

"Whatever, I can wear whatever the hell I want." She mumbled to herself. She walked in her room and shut the door.

Suddenly her mom walked in, "I wasn't done with you. I don't know who you think you are, walking around here like you own something." Shakia laid on her bed and stared at the ceiling. "I don't know what's been going on with you lately but whatever it is needs to change quickly or there will be consequences. I rebuke that rebellious spirit right now in Jesus' name." Shakia continued to look at the ceiling trying to ignore her mom.

"Your counselor called me today at work and scheduled me to meet with all of your teachers. Do you know what that is all about?"

"Naw… I couldn't tell you," She answered sarcastically. Her mom stared at her as if she wanted to pop her in her mouth.

"You know what? Since all of a sudden you think you're grown there's no TV, no phone, and no computer for a week." Her mom searched in her book bag and took her cell phone.

"Why you trippin'? I said I didn't know. You get on my nerves." Her mom walked out and slammed the door behind her. Shakia sat up on her bed and she began to go through her drawers looking for something to smoke.

"I can't stand that hoe." She muttered to herself. When she couldn't find anything to smoke she started to throw things all over her room until she grew tired. Shakia sat on her bed, filled with rage, and then started to scan her room until she spotted a pair of scissors lying on the floor. Shakia reached down to pick them up and placed then on the bed beside her. She just sat on her bed wondering what she could do to relieve her stress and anger. Her eyes wandered down to the scissors.

"Man … she get on my last nerve… but I got somethin' for her." Shakia picked up the scissors, dug them into her inner arm, then slid them down to her wrist. Blood rushed from her arm like a river going down stream. As the blood dripped on her pants, tears balled down her cheeks. Shakia glanced down at her arm and saw all the blood, then scrambled around her room searching for a towel to clean herself up. After wiping the blood up and changing clothes, she remembered she had a small bag of ecstasy taped under her bed. Shakia scurried under her bed in search of the pills. Once she found them she glanced at her wrist again and tied a grey du-rag around her cut. Next she locked her door, and popped the pills into her mouth. While she was waiting for the pills to start affecting her, she stood in the middle of her room. All of a sudden her legs began to weaken and she dropped to the floor. She crawled to a corner, then started to weep.

67

"God help me." She cried while blood was still coming from her arm. As Shakia was lying in the corner crying, the room began to get hot. She sat in the corner crying until she found the strength to crawl onto her bed. Once she got into her bed and closed her eyes the room started to cool down. As she was lying in her bed she thought about what she could do since her mom took her phone. When she reached for her house phone she started to get dizzy because of the ex still in her system.

After she got the phone, she dialed Jalissa's cell. "Hey Jalissa my ma took my cell so I will call you."

"Ok but I found out that one of my boys is throwin' a house party so you want to come or want to stay home?" Jalissa asked.

"I'm comin' but I got this ex in me so I'll call you once I wake up, 'cause I need to sleep this stuff off. What time you tryin' to roll out?"

"I probably leave my house around ten so I will be outside ya house at eleven 'cause I have some stuff to do."

"Ok... I'll see tonight."

"Oh Kia... wear somethin' sexy 'cause it's goin' to be niggas everywhere."

"Duhhh... I'm a sexy girl. But I'll see ya tonight. Holla."

~ ~ ~ ~ ~ ~ ~ ~

"Hey, Quincy, where are you?" Deon'te asked on the other side of the phone.

"I'm on Twenty Third Street makin' a lil paper."

"Ok, I'll be over in a minute 'cause I have to give you somethin'."

"Aight man I'll be standin' in front of the Pawn Shop." Quincy hung up his phone and leaned against the building. As he was waiting for Deon'te, a woman with torn clothes and ripped shoes stopped in front of him.

"What you sellin'?" the woman asked anxiously.

"What do you need?"

"Whatever you got I'll take it, just hurry up," she replied. She handed him the money then held out her shaking hands for the drugs. Quincy reached in his pocket and handed her a dime bag of weed. Once he handed it to her, she snatched the bag and quickly walked off. Right when he was about to walk in the pawn shop, a car stopped in front of the building. "Quincy!" a voice called. He turned around and noticed the car looked familiar. The car door opened and Ricky stepped out with a disappointed look on his face.

"What you doin' on this side of town?" Quincy asked with a grin on his face. Ricky walked over to the sidewalk, then leaned against his car. "Don't worry 'bout me. I saw what you just did."

"What are you talkin' 'bout?" Quincy said with an innocent look on his face.

"Dawg... don't play dumb with me. You just handed that woman some drugs!" Ricky exclaimed angrily.

"Man... don't come at me with that. I'm doin' what I do and what I do has nothin' to do with you."

"What do you mean what you do has nothin' to do with me. You're my best friend and I don't want to see you mess yaself up over stupid stuff." Quincy looked down the street wondering when Deon'te was going to pull up.

"Come on, Quincy, you have too much in ya future to do somethin' crazy like this." Quincy smacked his teeth and looked down at his shoes acting as if he didn't care to hear what Ricky was saying.

"Well... I need money and this is the only way I can work when I want to." Quincy said.

"What you talkin' 'bout? Ricky said, "You know how stupid you sound?"

69

"You're not me;" Quincy yelled, "ya people give you money. I don't have time for a real job and plus I make three times as much money sellin' then I would workin' at a fast food place."

"Quincy listen to me, you're not bein' smart. This is not the way to go. Ya lil friend Deon'te is makin' this lifestyle seem like roses but it's not."

"I'm tired of havin' this conversation, just let me do what I do."

"No… I'm not. God doesn't want me to give up on you."

"Man don't start with that church stuff. If God cared 'bout me I wouldn't have problems."

"What problems? Do you know ya future is laid out for you? All you have to do is walk the right path and trust in God." Quincy looked at his watch, and down the street searching for Deon'te.

"You still have to come to church with me 'cause I went with you that night."

"I don't think I can go to church right now 'cause I gave up on God, 'cause it seems to me that he gave up on me."

Ricky just stood in silence and in shock after hearing what Quincy said. "Umm… I'll be at ya house on Sunday to pick you up for church," Ricky said as he was getting into his car. Once he was settled in the car, Ricky drove off. After he left, Deon'te pulled in front of the Pawn Shop. Quincy walked over to the car then got in the passenger's seat.

"What's up…what do you need to give me?" Deon'te reached in the back seat and grabbed a brown bag and placed it in the dashboard of his car. "What's that?" Quincy asked.

"Get it… It's somethin' I want you to have 'cause you need it out here when you sellin'." Quincy grabbed the bag and peeked in, then quickly closed it.

70

"Naw... I can't take this. I don't need it."

"What you scared of boy? Take this." Deon'te snatched the bag and pulled the gun out.

"You need this 'cause its some crazy niggas out there." Quincy slowly reached for the gun and placed it on his lap.

"Dawg...I don't know 'bout a gun. The drugs were pushin' it but a gun, that's over the limit."

"Stop bein' a punk and take that." Quincy held the gun in his hand and studied it from end to end. "Man, I don't know 'bout this dawg. I was doin' fine without it."

"How long do you think you goin' to be lucky?" Deon'te asked sarcastically.

"Is this thing on safety lock?" Quincy asked.

"Of course. Why would it not be? It's not in use?" he answered. Quincy put the gun into his pants and laid his head back against the headrest. "Oh, do you want to go with me to a party?" Quincy looked out of the car window and noticed there was no one walking the streets.

"Nobody is out today... I'll go with you." Deon'te started the car and took off down the street.

"Well, that's where I'm goin' now. I want to get there early 'cause I want to holla at that girl Jalissa. Oh... and she got a lil underclassman friend."

"I don't want no underclassman... Is she a freak?" Deon'te chuckled to himself, "That's all you worried 'bout you lil horny bastard."

"That wasn't the answer I wanted. Is she a freak?" Deon'te took his eyes off the road and looked out of the window for a quick second. "Yea...Jalissa said she was, plus I heard from other people that Jalissa turned her out."

"Dang she must be a super freak. That's what I'm talkin' 'bout, tell ya girl Jalissa to put me down with her." Deon'te shook his head okay and reached into the ash tray to pull out a nickel bag of weed. Once Deon'te put the bag on the dashboard, Quincy reached into his pocket and pulled out a lighter.

"I need this 'cause my dad has been trippin' over stupid stuff lately." "Well... hurry up and roll that blunt." Once the blunt was ready Quincy put it in Deon'te's hand and then lit it.

"Are you goin' to college or are you goin' to become a professional hustla like me?" Deon'te asked as he took a puff and passed it to Quincy. Quincy took the blunt as he stared at him as if he had just threatened his mom.

"Nigga you must be crazy, of course I'm goin' to college. I'm gettin' the hell out of here. I was just sellin' 'cause I need money in my pockets," Quincy exclaimed. Deon'te looked at him in surprise and glanced at the time.

"How far is this party?" Quincy asked.

"It's right around this corner." he answered as he reached for the blunt then threw it out of the window. Once they pulled up to the house they stepped out of the car as if they were the badest boys on the block. Quincy followed Deon'te into the house and down to the basement where the party was being held. When Quincy stepped off the last step he looked up and saw some people dancing, some posted on the wall drinking, and others in another room playing a PlayStaion2.

"Do you see ya friend Jalissa?"

"Naw... she might be dancin'....There she is, follow me." Quincy followed Deon'te across the room until he stopped behind Jalissa. He slapped her on her butt, and then she turned quickly to see who it was. "Hey girl...what you been up to...'cause you stopped callin' me," Deon'te said as he put his arm around her shoulder. "Nigga... you know I've been busy and I don't make house calls," she answered.

"What are you talkin' 'bout? I didn't ask you all that... oh my bad. This is my boy Quincy."

"I know who he is," Jalissa said flirtatiously as she scanned Quincy from head to toe. Jalissa looked over his shoulder and saw Shakia dancing with a boy.

"Shakia...Shakia," she called. Shakia looked up searching the room to see who was calling her.

"Shakia, come here." Once Shakia saw Jalissa motioning her to come over, she casually made her way towards Jalissa.

"Is that the underclassman?" Deon'te asked in curiosity. Jalissa nodded her head as Shakia walked up.

"What's up?" she asked. As Shakia walked up. Quincy's eyes widened when he saw her. He was surprised at how grown she looked, she was wearing a strapless black shirt, skin tight blue jeans, knee high stiletto boots, and silver jewelry dangling from her neck and ears. Quincy stared at Shakia as if he wanted to marry her. While he was staring at her, Jalissa pulled Shakia towards her and whispered in her ear.

"You need to get with this boy 'cause one he is sexy as hell and two he is the best balla on the basketball team." Suddenly Quincy walked over to Shakia. He put his arm around her shoulder and slowly guided her away from Jalissa.

"So what's ya name?" Quincy asked as they walked in the room. "Shakia, what's yours?"

"Mine is Quincy, but you can call me Q." Once they got in the room they sat on the couch while two boys were playing the PlayStation2. After they got settled on the couch someone turned the lights off and everyone in the dancing room started cheering.

"You want to dance?" Shakia asked him with her hand on his thigh. Quincy glanced at her hand on his leg, quickly stood up, and led her to the dancing room. As they were walking onto the dance floor, Shakia stopped walking and guided him to an open space on the wall. Quincy posted against the wall while

Shakia began to grind on him. While she was dancing on him, she could feel his hand sliding up and down her waist. The way she was dancing on him, Quincy couldn't help but touch her. Just when Shakia was getting started, the DJ switched the record to a slow song. Everyone in the room quickly grabbed a partner, dancing to the music. Quincy took Shakia by the hand and led her back into the room with the boys still playing the PlayStation2. Shakia sat on the couch.

"I'll be back...I'm goin' to get us some drinks," Quincy said as he walked out of the door. She just sat on the couch and stared at the game the boys were playing. All of a sudden she started to think about the scripture her mom read to her about disobedience. *My people are destroyed for lack of knowledge. Because you have rejected knowledge I also will reject you from being priest for me; because you have forgotten the law of your God. I also will forget your children. Hosea 4:6*

"Shakia, you ok?" Quincy asked standing in front of her holding to Smirnoffs. "Yea...I was just in a daze."

Quincy sat down beside her on the couch, scooting closer to her while he handed her a Smirnoff. "So... how old are you?" he asked, taking a sip of his drink.

"Fifteen, but that shouldn't matter."

Quincy glanced at her chest, "The hell it don't. Like everybody says age ain't nothin' but some numbers."

Shakia rolled her eyes and took a sip of the Smirnoff. "You don't know how many niggas told me that."

Quincy placed his drink on the floor and put his hand on Shakia's leg. "You know what ... You are the finest girl I talk to and you look sexy as hell," he said lustfully as he started to kiss her on her neck. Shakia closed her eye, starting to get butterflies in her stomach. While he continued to kiss her neck, he slowly put his hands underneath her shirt. Suddenly Deon'te walked in the room with Jalissa clinging to his arm. He slowly walked behind the couch trying not to make too much noise. He leaned forward, then whispered, "I'll be back in about thirty or forty-five minutes. Me and Jalissa are goin' to handle some buisness."

Quincy stopped kissing Shakia, checking his pockets. "Do you have another rubber on you?" Deon'te reached into his pocket and pulled out a rubber and dropped it into Quincy's hand. While Shakia waited for Quincy, she drank the rest of her Smirnoff. Jalissa glanced at her, walking over and leaning over beside her.

"Don't worry 'bout anything. Just relax and let it happen," she told her. Shakia looked at her with a confused look.

"What you talkin' 'bout...let what happen?" asked Shakia. Jalissa walked back toward Deon'te, but as she was walking she winked at Shakia. After Jalissa winked, Shakia remembered another scripture. *A worthless person, a wicked man walks with a perverse mouth; He winks with his eyes, he shuffles his feet, he points with his fingers. Proverbs 6:12-13.* Quincy faced Shakia, smiling.

"Well... me and Jalissa will see y'all two later." Deon'te said as he and Jalissa walked out.

"Now...where did we leave off," Quincy said as he leaned forward to kiss Shakia. He started to kiss her on her neck again hoping the mood would still be the same. As he was kissing on her he started to rub her legs. Shakia just sat with eyes closed imagining things that they could be doing. Suddenly Quincy stopped and started to look around trying to find a place he could take her.

"Let's get away from all these people," he suggested as he continued to scan the room until he saw two double doors in the back of the room. Quincy stood up, took Shakia by the hand, and led her into the room. While Shakia was walking in the room her mind was telling her not to go in the room with him, but she ignored her thought and continued into the room. After they got into the room they looked around and figured that it was a guest room. Shakia sat on the bed, took her boots off, and laid back. When Quincy saw that she was getting comfortable, he laid on the other side of the bed beside her. He reached for her hand, then kissed it. "I like you Shakia...you different from the other girls."

"Nigga stop lyin'...I'm just like every other girl out there."

"No...you carry yaself different," he said as he stroked her face with his fingers. Shakia blushed as Quincy started to kiss her. He slowly moved his hand under her shirt, loosened her bra, and with his other hand, unbuttoned her jeans, Shakia didn't stop him because the temptation was too great to fight. Quincy rolled on top of her as he kicked his shoes off. As they continued to kiss, Shakia could hear her mom saying *"Make good choices."* Quincy unbuttoned his pants forgetting the condom Deon'te had given him.

Temptation - Proverbs 2:10-14
When wisdom enters your heart, And knowledge is pleasant to your soul, Discretion will preserve you; Understanding will keep you, To deliver you from the way of evil, From the man who speaks perverse things, From those who leave the paths of uprightness to walk in the ways of darkness; Who rejoice in doing evil, And delight in the perversity of the wicked.

~ Chapter Six~

THREE WEEKS LATER...

THREE WEEKS LATER...

"Shakia, open the door...I can't help you if you don't open the door," The school nurse shouted outside the bathroom door. Shakia was on her knees bent over the toilet throwing up.

"Open the door or I'm going to call your mom." Shakia scooted away from the toilet and then leaned against the wall. She took two deep breaths, looking at the door. The nurse knocked on the door.

"Sweetie, open the door please." Shakia slowly got on her feet to open the door. The nurse rushed in the bathroom, taking her temperature and feeling her forehead. Shakia sat down on the toilet leaning over in tears.

"You don't have a fever and I doubt you have a stomach virus." The nurse stepped back and folded her arms wondering what could be the problem.

"Have you been having sex?" Shakia looked up at her then slowly lowered her head in shame without saying a word.

"I guess that is a yes...well, have you been using protection?" Shakia lifted her head as her eyes widened.

"Are you tryin' to say I'm pregnant?" Shakia asked as tears rolled down her cheeks.

The nurse knelt beside her, "Sweetie, I'm not saying you are but you need to tell your mom you need to get a pregnancy test."

"I'm not tellin' my mom I might be pregnant...do you know what she would do to me?" The nurse put her arm around Shakia's shoulder trying to comfort her.

"Do you want me to call her and talk with her about the situation?" Shakia wiped her eyes then shrieked, "No...you don't know my mom...it will hurt her. I'll tell her." As Shakia stood up, the nurse went to her office and brought back a pass.

"Here is a pass to class...don't forget to tell your mom."

Shakia grabbed the pass and rushed out of the door and down the hallway towards Jalissa's class. While she was walking, tears started to roll down her cheek. Sidney and Ricky were walking towards her hand-in-hand.

"Hey, Shakia." Sidney called. When Shakia heard Sidney speak to her she quickly wiped her eyes so Sidney could not tell she was crying. Once they were face-to-face, Sidney noticed that Shakia's eyes were red.

"What's wrong? It looks like you've been cryin'." Shakia just stood in front of them with her head down.

Sidney looked at Ricky, "I'll catch up with you later... no wait, I'll see you tonight at church." After he walked away Shakia lifted her head, "Y'all have dates at church?" Shakia asked. "Yeah...he has me goin' to church every Sunday and some Wednesdays for Bible study. Oh and you need to know ya dad is a good preacher."

"He can be a good preacher but not a good dad. He's so caught up in church he is never home."

"Do you even go to church anymore?"

Shakia glanced at her then said, "No...on Sunday mornin' I'm sleepin'."

"Well ...with all those parties you go to on Saturday nights." Shakia took a deep breath, "How do you know 'bout that?"

"Ya name is all over the school...and it's not a good one at that." Suddenly Shakia started to cry again.

"What's wrong with you...tell me?" She just stood there covering her face with her hand weeping. Sidney grabbed her by the arm and guided her to a deserted hallway by the gym.

"Tell me what's wrong...I can't help you if you don't tell me." Shakia looked at Sidney and then hugged her.

"Shakia, tell me what is goin' on."

While they were hugging, Shakia muttered, "I

might…" Sidney stepped back and places her hands on her shoulders.

"You might what?"

Shakia wiped her nose and said, "I might be pregnant." Once she said that she started to cry even harder.

Sidney stared at her in shock, "What!" She hugged Shakia as she cried on her shoulder.

"You need to tell ya mom." Shakia looked at her with her wet red eyes.

"I'm not tellin' her…do you know how that would make me and my family look. My dad is a pastor and my mom is a respected woman. How would that look?"

"Well…you shoulda thought about that before you opened ya legs. It seems to me you weren't thinkin' at all."

"I don't know what to do…I'm scared." Sidney hugged her then looked her in the eyes.

"Why you bein' so nice to me? I did you and the girls wrong," Shakia replied.

"Well, have you read the story in the Bible 'bout Saul not likin' David? But Saul had a son named Jonathan who was David's friend. Even though Jonathan's dad did not like Saul, Jonathan still stuck with him through all his trials."

"You learned a lot at church."

"Yeah you can say that…my new boo has me listenin' to ya dad and everything."

"Well… thanks for bein' a good friend even though I wasn't one to you."

"Call me if you need anything. We made a promise long ago to be best friends forever and I never will break it. So if you have any problems or just need to talk call me like you used to do. I need to go get my things cause there is five minutes of school left." Sidney hugged her again and walked off. Once she was gone Shakia looked at the school clock and went to her locker. Once she got her things she headed towards Jalissa's class. While she was walking she started to think of who the father could be. When she got to Jalissa's class she looked in the window trying to get Jalissa's attention. Suddenly the bell rang and the students rushed into the hall. Jalissa walked out and saw Shakia leaning on the wall.

"Hey...why you meet me over here?"

"Is Mercedes and Ashley ridin' with you today?" Shakia asked ignoring Jalissa's question.

"No, but I have to meet them at the car."

"Good, 'cause you have to take me to get somethin' at the store." They walked to the main hallway towards the car. Quincy came up behind Shakia and grabbed her from behind.

"Hey, baby I haven't seen you all day."

"I've been in the nurse's office," she answered.

"Meet me at the car. I have to do somethin' real quick," Jalissa said as she pushed her way though the crowded halls.

"So when we goin' to go on another date," Quincy asked putting his hands on her waist.

"I guess whenever you call me...but I can't go anywhere for a couple of days 'cause I have some personal things I have to take care of."

"Ok, call me tonight so we can plan." He kissed her on the cheek, then walked off into the crowd of students. Once Shakia got outside she scanned the parking lot for Jalissa's car. When she spotted the car she saw Mercedes and Ashley standing by it. As she was walking toward the car Jalissa came up beside her.

"Are you ok... 'cause you look a lil shook," Jalissa exclaimed coming up beside her.

"I'll tell you 'bout it once we get settled in the car." Mercedes and Ashley were sitting on the hood of the car waiting for Jalissa.

"It took you long enough to get out here," Mercedes said sarcastically. "My bad I had to go make my runs. Then Shakia was talkin' to her new boo," Jalissa replied.

"Who's her new boo...I'm surprised a boy would even want her," Mercedes said jealously.

"Look chick don't start with me today I'm not in the mood for ya smart comments," Shakia shouted as she got in the car.

While she was sitting in the car she heard Jalissa say, "Why do you keep messin' with her, she ain't do nothin' to you."

"Ever since she got in the picture you seem to have forgotten 'bout me and you," Mercedes exclaimed.

"Ok that's enough of that subject...do you have the stuff?" Ashley asked interrupting their conversation. "Yeah...I got it, where is my money?"

As Shakia was eaves dropping on their conversation, she saw Ashley hand Jalissa some money, then Jalissa tossed her a bag of pills. "Don't have too much fun with those," Jalissa said playfully. Mercedes and Ashley smiled and casually walked away. Jalissa got in the car and started it.

"What did you give em'?" Shakia asked.

"Nothin' important," Jalissa answered as she drove off down the street.

"Jalissa, if I tell you somethin' you have to promise me you won't say anything to anybody."

"Yeah...of course what's wrong?" Shakia took a deep breath then sighed.

"I think I'm pregnant ... I was in the nurse's office throwin' up."

"You sure...you could've just eaten somethin' bad."

"No I doubt it was food, that's why I need you to take me to the store so I can buy a pregnancy test."

"We can go to the pharmacy 'round the corner." Once they got to the pharmacy, Shakia went straight to the aisle with the feminine products. As she was scanning the shelves for the pregnancy test, Jalissa stood beside her holding two pregnancy tests in her hand.

"Get this kind 'cause it tell you ya results in less than two hours," Jalissa suggested.

"How you know?"

"Because first of all I read the box and second of all I used it before and my results came back in an hour."

"Why you have two?"

"You always get two so you know ya results are hundred percent right." Shakia grabbed the boxes then went to the cash register. When she placed the two tests on the counter the cashier shook her head in disappointment.

"How old are you?" the cashier asked in curiosity.

"Fifteen."

"I hope these aren't for you." Shakia searched in her purse for some money.

"Naw these are for my mom...she didn't feel like comin' in the store." The cashier glanced at her with a smirk and rang up the items.

"It's goin' to be $36.43." Right when Shakia was about to hand the cashier the money, Jalissa pulled her arm back.

"I got it...you need to save ya money," Jalissa assured. As they were getting in the car Jalissa asked, "Where are you goin' to do them?"

"We can go to my house. My mom doesn't get home until six and it's only three," Shakia suggested. Jalissa drove off headed towards Shakia's house. While they were driving, Shakia looked at the pregnancy test in the bag.

"Did you used to be pregnant?" Shakia asked. Jalissa glanced at her, hesitating before she answered.

"Yeah...but I had to get rid of it."

"Why...you didn't have to do anything."

"Kia, how would that look...me walkin' around the school with a big stomach?"

"So you got an abortion?"

"Hell yeah, I wasn't ready for no kid."

"Didn't you feel bad after you did it?"

"Yeah, I cried for a lil while but I realize I had to do what I had to do and life goes on. But bein' pregnant once never stopped me from doin' what I was doin'. I just started usin' protection." Jalissa parked at the corner next to Shakia's house and they got out and walked towards the house. Once they got in the room Shakia took out one of the tests, sat on the bed, and read the instructions.

When Jalissa saw her reading the instructions she rolled her eyes and said, "Let me save you some time. First, pee in a cup. Then let the test sit in the pee until you get your positive or negative sign." Shakia took a deep breath, went to the bathroom, and got a medicine cup from behind the mirror. She followed Jalissa's instructions and urinated in the cup. While Shakia was in the bathroom, Jalissa was in her room smoking a blunt. After Shakia did what Jalissa said, she walked back into her room and when she opened her door the room was half filled with smoke.

"What you doin'? Don't get high in my room...my ma will smell it when she gets home." Jalissa took a puff then blew out the smoke from the side of her mouth.

"Nigga stop worryin'...that's ya problem you worry 'bout everything. Just sit by me and help me smoke this 'cause you need somethin' to do while you wait." Shakia stood by her dresser and folded her arms.

"You just goin' to stand there or are you goin' to smoke with me?" Jalissa exclaimed. She sat down beside her on the bed and reached for the blunt. "What should I do if I'm pregnant?" Shakia asked as she took two puffs of the blunt.

"I think you need to do what you want to do. If you think you can handle a baby then have it, but if you don't want to have it then get rid of it." Shakia took two more puffs then passed the blunt to Jalissa.

"Personally, I don't think you should have a baby 'cause it's goin' to mess up that sexy shape of yours." Shakia chuckled to herself then laid her head on Jalissa's shoulder. Jalissa put her hand on her leg and kissed her on her forehead.

"I'm scared," Shakia said.

"It's goin' to be ok. Do you know who the daddy might be?"

Shakia thought to herself for a moment then lifted her head. "Quincy."

"What 'bout Quincy?" Jalissa asked.

"I remember at the party when we first met we had sex and I don't remember him strappin' up." Suddenly tears began to fall from Shakia's eyes. Jalissa heard her sniff, "Sweetie, it's goin' to be fine. If you don't want it, I'll take you to go get an abortion."

"No...I'm scared...somethin' told me not to even go in that room with him."

"Stop trippin', accidents happen." Jalissa stroked Shakia's face with her fingers, then lifted her head looking into her eyes. Suddenly, just when they were about to kiss, Shakia's mom burst threw the door.

"Shakia what is all this smoke..." her mom shouted as she stood in the doorway in shock.

"What are y'all doing?" her mom asked. Shakia glanced at Jalissa, then she quickly stood up.

"Nothin'." Her mom scanned the room until she saw the blunt lying on one of Shakia's school books. She walked into the room and picked up the blunt.

"What is this? This doesn't look like *nothin'* to me." Jalissa glanced over at Shakia. She tried to walk out of the room but Shakia's mom stepped in the way.

"I don't want to see you at my house again or near my child…and if I catch you talking to her I swear to God I'll get a restraining order on you."

Jalissa rolled her eyes and said, "Whatever." As she was walking out the door she winked at Shakia while her mom wasn't looking and then left. Once her mom heard the front door shut she lit into Shakia.

"What in the world did you think you were doin? And were you about to kiss her?" Shakia just stood there with her head down in shame.

"None of that is acceptable in this house. I knew something was going on with you when you started to change the style of your clothes and when your grades went down." As Shakia was standing there a tear dropped from her eye to the floor.

"You let some girl come into your life and start hell… there is no need for you to cry now. Why did you let the devil tell you bein' with a girl wasn't wrong? You know **Leviticus 18:22** says, "**You shall not lie with a male as with a female. It is an abomination.**" Then not only were you involved with a girl but you are doin' drugs too. Do you know drugs can throw you all off physically. Drugs are like you're killing yourself slowly. Just wait until your dad gets home so he can deal with you cause I can't even look at you right now."

"He's never at home anyway so why should I care," Shakia said under her breath. Shakia lifted her head and saw all the disappointment in her mom's face.

"Ma, I'm sorry. I just wanted to try somethin' different," she replied as she wiped her nose.

"You wanted to try something different? Why would you try this knowing that it's wrong? You don't even have to answer that 'cause I already know...you wanted to be like the other kids. Now let me tell you something what is in the dark will soon come into the light." She stormed out of the room and slammed the door. Shakia glanced at herself in the mirror, then laid on her bed weeping. Shortly after, Shakia's mom returned and went to Shakia's bathroom to search the closet for drugs that she may have hidden. Suddenly she looked on the counter and saw the pregnancy test sitting in the urine. Seeing the test read positive, she sat on the toilet and cried.

"God why...why didn't I see any of this before?" After she got herself together she walked out of the bathroom and slowly opened Shakia's door. Shakia sat up on her bed and looked at her mom.

"You've been having sex, too?" her mom shouted as she held up the test results. Shakia's mouth dropped when she saw her mom holding the test.

"Ma I'm sorry."

"I don't want to hear it. Do you want to know what your result is? I have one word for you positive. When have you had sex and who have you done it with?" Shakia laid on her bed then put her face in her pillows and cried. When her mom saw how hurt she was she sat on the edge of the bed and comforted her daughter.

"Ma, leave me alone." Shakia yelled. Her mom hugged her, kissing her on her forehead.

"We're goin' to get through this with God's help.

~ ~ ~ ~ ~ ~ ~ ~

"What's up dad...where's my mom?" Quincy asked his dad as he walked into the kitchen. His dad was sitting on the

87

couch in the living room smoking a cigarette and drinking a forty-ounce Corona. "Ya mom is at work, somewhere you need to be." Quincy ignored his dad's sarcastic comment and headed towards the refrigerator. He opened the refrigerator door and took out sandwich meat, and a soda. His dad took a sip of his beer, then stood in the kitchen doorway and watched Quincy make his sandwich.

"I should make you pay for that, since you don't help pay for anything." His dad walked over to the refrigerator and slammed the door. Quincy continued to ignore his dad's comment while he made his sandwich. His dad began to scan him up and down.

"Who bought you new clothes? 'Cause I know I didn't and I know ya ma didn't either. And you ain't got a job," his dad responded with curiosity. Quincy grabbed his sandwich and soda, trying to walk out of the kitchen without speaking to his dad. Right when Quincy was about to walk out his dad put his arm across the doorway.

"Do you hear me talkin' to you boy?" He glanced at his dad, placed his food on the counter, and then sat on the counter.

"I bought these clothes and I don't think you should worry about where I get my stuff from cause you don't buy anything." His dad drank the rest of his beer and slammed the bottle on the counter.

"Look boy, who you think ya talkin' to…I'm not ya friend. If you don' t tell me where you got em' I'm goin' to have to say you stole em'….'cause one, you don't have a job and two, you don't have any money to even help 'round the house." Quincy put his head down, took a deep breath, and then jumped off the counter.

"You never have anything good to say to me. You always put me down, I bet you don't even like me… but you know what...I don't care. Once I graduate I'm out of here and I don't want to have anything to do with you." Quincy reached into his pocket and pulled out a two-inch thick wad of money with hundreds on the top. Once his dad saw the wad of money, his eyes widened. "Here, you want some money?" Quincy asked as he flipped through the bills. He threw three hundred dollar bills at his dad's chest and stormed past him.

Suddenly when Quincy walked into the living room his mom came through the front door, "I'm home." She greeted slowly shutting the door behind her.

Quincy went to greet his mom, "Hey ma."

"Hey sweetie... how was your day?"

"It was ok until I got home...you know ya husband can't stop naggin'." Quincy leaned against the wall and reached into his pocket again. "Here ma...I want you to have this." He handed her two hundred dollars and then headed to his room.

"Wait... where did this money come from?" his mom asked as his dad slowly walked in the room and sat down.

"Don't worry 'bout that...I just want you to buy yaself somethin'...you always buy stuff for me but now I want you to get yaself somethin'."

"Just tell me were you got this money," she exclaimed.

"If you don't stop questionin' him and take the money...Why you always have to ask a question...he gave you money so take it," his dad responded angrily.

"I just want to know where he is getting this money from because he doesn't have a job," she replied.

"Don't talk back to me, woman... I didn't tell you to answer me. Just take the money and leave it at that."

"Nigga...I'm tired of you talkin' to my mom like she's a dog." Quincy shouted angrily.

"I can talk to her and you any way I want. I'm the man of this house."

"You not a man…you just call yaself one. You haven't paid a single bill…let alone provide me with anything for three years. My mom has been strugglin' everyday tryin' to pay the bills and take care of a teenage boy. And she has to come home to a drunken man who doesn't even show her any kind of appreciation."

His dad stood up from his seat and walked over to Quincy with his fist balled up. "Who in the hell do you think you talkin' to like that?" his dad yelled as he pushed Quincy. Quincy stepped in his dad's face and his mom hopped between them.

"Y'all stop."

"Woman, move…he wants to act like a man let him get beat like a man." His dad pushed her against the wall and charged at Quincy. Quincy pushed his dad against the wall and wrapped his left hand around his neck while he held up his right hand ready to punch him until he looked at his dad and saw fear in his eyes. He glanced over his shoulder and saw his mom leaning against the wall in tears. He lowered his fist and slowly stepped back, glaring at his dad with fire in his eyes. He continued to walk backwards and took one more glance at his mom before he quickly walked out of the front door, slamming it behind him. When he got outside he reached into his back pocket and pulled out a pack of cigarettes and his cell phone. He lit the cigarette and started to smoke and as he was smoking, he called Ricky on his phone.

"Hey, Ricky, come pick me up at my house."

"Aight I'll be there in five minutes…what's goin' on? You sound mad."

"I'll tell you when you get here... I'll be at the end of my street waitin'," Quincy added.

"Ok."

Quincy hung up the phone and started to walk down to the end of the street. While he was walking he continued to smoke then he stopped and sat on the corner of the street. As he was sitting there, he began to think about how he wanted to move out of his house.

Suddenly Deon'te rolled down his car window, "Hey... what you doin' on the corner...you look like you just lost ya best friend." Quincy slowly looked at Deon'te and tossed his cigarette onto the ground. "Naw...it ain't like that I'm just waitin' for somebody to pick me up," he replied. "Oh...well, I'll holla at you later 'cause I have to go make a drop." "Ok, I'll holla." Quincy said as he dialed Ricky's number on his phone. Deon'te drove off and Quincy put the phone to his ear.

"Hey, Ricky, you almost here? He asked. "Yeah, I'm comin' 'round the corner now." Quincy hung up his phone as Ricky pulled up in front of him. Once he got in the car, Ricky noticed something was wrong with Quincy. "Hey man...what's goin' on?" Ricky asked as he drove off. Quincy glanced out of the car window, then at Ricky. "Me and my dad got into a fight...I had to leave before I pulled this out on him." Quincy said as he lifted his shirt showing Ricky the gun. "Where you get a gun from?"

"You already know who gave it to me... but on a serious note I can't live with that man anymore... 'cause I might do somethin' crazy."

"Why do you let him upset you? That's the problem... just ignore him?"

"It's not that... he put his hands on my mom and I'm tired of him disrespectin' her."

"Why did he put his hand on her?"

"The nigga crazy! It all started when my dad was trippin' over money and he wanted to know how I got new clothes, so I just gave him some but I didn't tell him where I got it. Then my mom got home and I just handed her two hundred dollars."

"So that's not tellin' me why ya dad put his hands on ya mom."

"Then my mom started askin' me where I got the money from. After that my dad jumped in and told her not to ask where I got it from. That's how it all started."

"Do you know why you goin' through a lot of stuff?"

"Naw... why don't you tell me Miss Cleo," Quincy said sarcastically. Ricky glanced at him and scowled. "I'm goin' to ignore that...but like I was sayin' you havin' so many problems 'cause you runnin' away from God." Before Ricky could finish Quincy interrupted, "Man...God don't want me to do nothin'. He hasn't said anything to me."

"You're just not listenin'. I'm tryin' to tell you don't run from him... 'cause you goin' to keep havin' problems until you surrender to him." Quincy shook his head with a smirk on his face, "Stop tryin' to preach to me..."

"You know what's wrong with you? You have too much pride Jeremiah 50:32 says, *"The most proud shall stumble and fall, and no one will raise him up; I will kindle a fire in his cities. And it will devour all around him."*

"What are you tryin' to do? Scare me?.. well it's not workin'," Quincy replied. Ricky chuckled to himself, "Naw...I'm just tryin' to let you know what God's word says." Quincy leaned his head back against the seat.

"Have you noticed that things are starting to go wrong in your life?" Ricky asked. Quincy closed his eyes before he glared at Ricky, "Are you tryin' to tell me God is punishin' me?"

"No... he's not punishin' you, he's tryin' to push you towards him. Until you decide to choose him instead of the world you're goin' to continue to have problems." Suddenly Quincy's phone rang it was Deon'te.

"Who is it?" Ricky asked.

"Deon'te... should I pick up?"

"No...don't pick up...that's another thing that is throwin' you off course."

"Deon'te is just tryin' to help me out."

Ricky burst out in laughter, "You think he's tryin' to help...he is influencin' you to smoke and do drugs. Not just do drugs but sell em'. I don't consider that helpin'."

"The drugs help me get my mind off of my problems and it helps me relax and sellin' em' keeps money in my pocket."

"You don't have to turn to drugs cause you have problems or need to relax." Quincy turned on the radio trying to bring the conversation to an end. Ricky glanced over at him then quickly turned it off.

"Stop tryin' to avoid this conversation. You're goin' to listen to me," Ricky fussed. Suddenly, Quincy's phone rang again. "Hello," he answered. While he was waiting for the person to answer, he heard a girl sniffling and weeping.

"Hello...who is this?...Hello." He answered.

"Quincy...this is Shakia."

"Hey baby what's wrong...are you cryin'?"

"I'm...I'm..."

"You what...tell me...what's goin' on?"

Ricky looked at Quincy in curiosity.

"What's goin' on?"

Quincy waved his arm for Ricky to be quiet.

"Shakia baby what's wrong?"

"I'm ...pregnant and it's yours."

Quincy's mouth dropped, "Are you sure you're pregnant and are you sure it's mine?" He heard Shakia crying even harder. "I...I took a pregnancy test and it came back positive...remember at the party you didn't put on a rubber and you the last boy I did it with." Quincy put his head down between his legs, then came up quickly. "Does anybody else know?"

"Yeah my ma and a girl named Sidney."

"Ya mom knows...why you tell her?"

"I didn't…she came home and saw it in my bathroom."

"Dang… you need to get rid of it…I'm not…I mean we can't take care of a baby." Once Quincy said "baby" Ricky's eyes widened and he slowly pulled over to the side of the road.

"I don't know if my ma will let me get one… 'cause she doesn't believe in abortion." Quincy grew angry, "It doesn't matter what ya mom believes in…it's your body, you can do whatever you want with it."

"I don't even know if I want to have an abortion…I'm scared. I don't know what to do." Quincy thought to himself for a moment. "Do you want to get an abortion?" he asked her.

"I don't know… I need to think about what I need to do."

"Well… are you at home?"

"Yeah…but I'm on lock down so I guess I will have to talk to you at school."

"Aight… if you need anything call me."

"Ok," she said as she hung up the phone. Quincy put his phone in his pocket and looked at Ricky. "I got her pregnant…I can't believe I got her pregnant."

"Who?" Ricky exclaimed.

"A girl named Shakia. We met at a party…don't say anything to anybody."

"Did you say Shakia? …Her dad is the pastor of my church."

Homosexuality - Leviticus 20:13
If a man lies with a male as he lies with a woman, both have committed an abomination…

Pride - Ezekiel 35:13-15
Thus with your mouth you have boasted against Me and multiplied your words against Me; I have heard them. Thus says the Lord God: The whole earth will rejoice when I make you desolate. As you rejoiced because the inheritance of the house of Israel was desolated, so I will do to you; you shall be desolate…

~ Chapter Seven~

LATER THAT NIGHT...

LATER THAT NIGHT...

While Shakia was in her room waiting for her dad to get home, she sat on the floor in the pitch black, weeping. She stood up and turned on the lamp sitting on her dresser. When she was about to sit on her bed she spotted a pair of scissors lying next to the lamp. She grabbed the scissors and locked her room door. After she locked the door she stood in the middle of her room with tears bawling from her eyes. Suddenly she dug the scissors deep into her inner forearm and slowly slid them horizontally across her arm. The blood from her arm trickled onto her white socks. Shakia bit her bottom lip with tears running down her cheeks. She sat on her bed and dug the scissors in her arm again and slid them across her wrist again. Once she placed the scissors on the floor she searched her room for a towel. When she spotted a pink towel hanging off the edge of her bed, she grabbed it, and tended to her wounds. The blood stained parts of the towel; once she stopped bleeding she threw the towel under her bed so her mom would not find it. She laid on her bed and stared at the phone. She remembered her mom had put her on phone restriction but she paid her mom's demands no mind. When she picked up the phone she called Sidney.

"Hello," Sidney answered.

"Hey, Sidney, I need to talk to you," Shakia whispered.

"Who is this?"

"It's Shakia."

"Why whisperin'?"

Shakia ignored her question.

"I'm pregnant...and my mom came home and saw the pregnancy test I took sittin' on my bathroom counter."

"You serious...ya pregnant?"

"Yeah...and I still don't know what I'm gonna do."

"Have you figured out who the dad is?" Sidney asked in

curiosity. Shakia felt blood dripping down her arm again so she fetched the towel she threw under her bed.

"Do you know a boy named Quincy in the twelfth grade?"

"Yeah... I know him, that's my boyfriend's best friend," Sidney paused for a moment. "That's ya baby daddy." Shakia was silent for a second and answered in shame, "Yeah."

"What did ya ma say? Is she gonna make you have it?"

"I don't know ...but I don't wanna have a baby. Do you know what havin' a baby would do to my image?" Sidney smacked her teeth in disgust.

"Girl...why you worried 'bout your image? You need to slow ya roll."

"What you mean?...This was an accident."

"Oh..., so you think if you get an abortion then everything is goin' to be ok? If you get an abortion you're not learnin' ya lesson, you just goin' to keep actin' like a hoe."

"I ain't a hoe," Shakia replied aggressively.

"I didn't call you a hoe. I said you actin' like one. That girl Jalissa got you actin' like somethin' ya not," Sidney said. Shakia got quiet and listened to Sidney.

"Let me be honest with you... you know what I heard about ya so called friend Jalissa. She is bisexual; she finds underclassman girls and gets em' caught up. Like that girl Mercedes. I heard she use to be a quiet girl until she started talking to Jalissa." Shakia's eyes grew big when she heard Sidney mention Mercedes.

"Who told you all of this?" Shakia asked.

"I just heard it 'round school..."

"Why you tellin' me this 'he say she say' stuff...unless you talked to her yaself. Don't tell me 'bout that gossip," Shakia exclaimed.

"That's ya problem you don't want to listen," Sidney

replied. "Ok, can we please change the subject?" Shakia suggested with an attitude. "Whatever, I don't care."

"Do you think I should have this baby?"

"To be truly honest I think you should. Reason one is 'cause I don't think any baby should be killed; they have a right to live to. Reason two is 'cause you thought you were old enough to open ya legs, so then you must have thought you were old enough to take care of a baby." Shakia didn't say anything. She just lay on her bed and examining the cuts until she heard someone come in the house. She quickly stood up and peeked out of her bedroom door. When she heard her dad's voice she slowly shut the door so it would not make a lot of noise.

"Dang…my dad is home…I'm gonna call you or just talk to you at school."

"Ok, I'll talk to you later." Shakia quickly hung up the phone, and started pacing back and forth in her room. Suddenly, her mom yelled to her from downstairs, "Shakia come down here." Just when she was about to open her door she saw her wrist; she quickly scrambled through her room for a shirt to cover it up. Finally she found a light grey sweatshirt; she put it on and went down the steps. Once she got downstairs her mom and dad were both sitting on separate couches with their hands on their foreheads. As she was about to sit down she spotted the pregnancy test lying beside her dad's foot.

After she sat down there was complete silence for two minutes until her dad said, "What in the world were you thinking?" Shakia sat in the chair with her head down. "Do you have any idea what you just did to your future and this family?" he exclaimed. Her mom touched his leg trying to calm him.

"When did this happen? Look at me when I'm talking to you!" her dad demanded.

Shakia inhaled, then slowly exhaled. "I went to a party 'bout three weeks ago at somebody's house."

"What party...you didn't ask me about going to any party," Her mom replied.

"I...I snuck out when y'all were sleep." Her dad stomped his foot trying to control his anger.

"How many times have you snuck out?" he asked.

"I don't know."

"Who took you to this party?" her mom asked.

Shakia looked away from her mom then answered, "Ja...Jalissa." When she said that name her mom's eyes widened, then she picked up the test. "Because you decided to sneak out of the house and act grown, you're going to really have to grow up."

Her dad interrupted, "Not only are you pregnant but your mom told me she walked in on you and your so called friend kissing and to add to that she found a blunt in your room." Shakia glanced at her dad rolling her eyes.

"So you did three things you know are not acceptable in this house. The first one is having sex, the second is drugs, and the third is being sexually involved with a girl," Her dad added.

"What made you do these things? Did we do something wrong as parents?" Her mom asked as her eyes began to water. Shakia saw how hurt her mom was and tears started to fill her eyes, also. "Are you going to answer the question? What made you do this?" her dad said impatiently.

"I...I don't know. I wanted to be like the other kids. I wanted to experience what they did," she said as tears rolled down her eyes.

"Where did I go wrong?" her dad murmured to himself. When Shakia heard him say that she wiped her eyes and stared at her dad.

"You! Where did you go wrong? You were never home, you're always doin' somethin' for the church or out of town preachin' at some church. You didn't even raise me...I consider my mom as a single parent." Her dad stared at her in shock.

"Don't persecute me for bein' a man of God."

"I feel like I don't even have a dad. If you woulda sat me down and talked with me about boys, maybe I wouldn't be in this situation I'm in now. This is my first time really even talkin' with you. You never ask me how I'm doin' or how I feel 'cause ya never here. If I was mom I would tell you to move out and live at the church since that's where you are twenty four- seven." Her mom sat back in her seat with an open mouth in surprise at what her daughter was saying.

"How come you didn't tell me you felt this way?" her mom asked as a tear rolled down her cheek.

"'Cause I don't like tellin' people how I feel." She looked at her dad and said, "He's one of the reasons I snuck out 'cause he's never home and when he's not home I can't get caught."

"No…I'm not the reason you did anything, you had a choice and you made the wrong one," he exclaimed. Shakia quickly stood up and walked towards the stairs.

"Get back here!" her dad demanded. Shakia ignored him and stormed up the stairs slamming the door of her room behind her. She had so much anger built up inside her, suddenly she knocked everything on her dressers onto the floor. She went into her closet and threw her clothes all over her room trying to take out her anger on something. Her dad opened her door and her mom pushed her way past him trying to get to her daughter.

"Shakia calm down," she said as she grabbed her and hugged her. "Let me go!" she screamed. Her dad scanned the room until he spotted some clothes on the floor with price tags still on them. He walked over and picked them up. "What is this?" Her mom slowly let her go and walked over towards her husband.

"So this is how you've been getting those clothes."

"Yeah… I stole them; there was no other way for me to get 'em." Her dad leaned against the wall and slowly slid to his knees with his hands on his head. While Shakia was standing in the middle of her room her mom noticed a dark red stain on Shakia's sweat shirt.

"What is that?" her mom asked as she walked over and grabbed Shakia by the arm. She quickly yanked her arm back and put her arm behind her back.

"Let me see your arm," her mom demanded. She shook her head no, but her mom walked over and lifted her sleeve. Once her mom saw the cuts, she slowly stepped back and put her hand over her mouth. She ran out of the room to get some peroxide so she could tend to Shakia's arm.

"Oh... so you cut yaself, too?" her dad said in a calm voice. Her mom ran back in the room and pours the peroxide on her arm. Shakia pulled it back because the pain was unbearable.

"Give me your arm," her mom demanded. While her mom was tending to her, her dad was still by the wall shaking his head.

"My daughter's having a baby, doing drugs, stealing, and is now a cutter," he said to himself.

Shakia looked at him and said, "Do I have to have this baby?"

"Yes... you're not going to get an abortion. If you can lay there and have five minutes of sex then you can lay on a hospital bed for six hours in labor," her mom replied.

"Why? I don't want to...I'm not ready," Shakia cried.

"Well, I'm sorry. You're going to have to get ready."

The room was silent until Shakia tried to persuade her parents, "I promise I won't have sex, do drugs and that other stuff again. Please."

"Shakia, you're having that baby and that's the end of it."

~ ~ ~ ~ ~ ~ ~ ~ ~

While Ricky was driving, Quincy reclined his seat closing his eyes and thinking about Shakia.

101

"Quincy what are you gonna do?"

Quincy opened his eyes and said, "I don't know...I hope she gets an abortion 'cause I can't take care of a baby right now. If she has that baby it will mess up everything, no college will want me if they find out I have a baby."

Ricky pulled into a deserted parking lot then turned off the car. "Listen...if you're good enough to be drafted into the NBA, any college will find a way for you to play and take care of that baby," Ricky said. Quincy's cell phone rang but he pushed ignore.

"I think you seriously need to come to church with me," Ricky suggested. Quincy glanced at him with a wild look.

"Dude...you must be crazy. Ya pastor is Shakia's dad. What if she told em' I got her pregnant? I'm not showin' my face in that church."

"Man...they don't know you...I'm tellin' you, the only way ya gonna get through this storm is with God's help." Quincy turned his head towards the window and put his hands over his face. Suddenly his phone rang again; he looked to see who it was and it was Deon'te.

He pressed ignore again and said, "How do you know he doesn't know who I am...I'm in the newspaper all the time for basketball." Ricky banged his hand against the steering wheel in frustration.

"It doesn't matter if he knows you or not, church is for everyone. He's not even goin' to notice you 'cause it's so many people that come to church." Quincy thought to himself for a second; he thought about the problems he was having with his dad, Shakia, and hustling.

"Man...I don't know if the church thing is for me... I've done so much sin that I got a first class ticket to hell. I don't see why you think God even cares 'bout a person like me. I'm not a saint like you."

"Q, I sin, too. I've done things too, but I repented and that's somethin' you have to do...God will forgive you. *John 3:16* says, *for God so loved the world that he gave his only begotten son, so that whoever believes in him should not perish but have everlasting life.*"

"And what is that supposed to mean? You tellin' me this stuff like I know what it means."

Ricky smiled to himself and said, "That scripture means that God loved you, me, and everyone else so much that he sent his son Jesus to earth to save us from goin' to hell." Suddenly Quincy's phone rang again and it was Deon'te again.

"Hello!" Quincy answered.

"Yo...how come you not pickin' up ya phone?" Deon'te asked.

"I've been busy... I had some problems I had to deal with."

"Oh. Can you do me a favor?" Ricky put his head on the steering wheel.

"Uhhh!" Quincy glanced at Ricky then said, "Yeah... what is it?"

"I need you to come with me to make a drop. I have this dude that's putting up five G's and I will give you half if you do it with me."

Quincy sat his seat up then said, "So...if I do this with you, you'll give me twenty five hundred?" Quincy asked hesitant.

"Yeah dawg...I'm not gonna lie to you." Quincy glanced over at Ricky once more then said, "Yeah...I'll do it pick me up at the Pawn Shop on Twenty Third Street."

"Aight I'll be there in five minutes."

"Aight," Quincy said, hanging up the phone. Once he got off the phone Ricky lifted his head. "Who was that?" he asked. "That was Deon'te; he wants me to help him do somethin'. Can you drop me off at the Pawn Shop on Twenty Third Street?" Ricky studied him...

"For what? I heard you mention somethin' 'bout money. What's that about?" Quincy put his fingers between his eyes, "Nothin'…he said he'll give me twenty five hundred if I help him do somethin'."

"Why is he givin' you that much money?"

Quincy laughed to himself, "Look twenty one questions…he just needs me to help him drop somethin' off." Ricky shook his head and said, "Naw…that don't sound right to me. You need to let that dude go. Stop talkin' to him."

"That's my boy. He asked me to do him a favor, so I'm goin' to do it." Ricky smacked his teeth, "*John 15:13* says, *Greater love has no one than this, that to lay down one's life for his friends.* Now do you honestly think Deon'te would give his life for you?"

"Dude…that's my boy, of course he got my back and how many times have you read the Bible. You can quote every scripture." Ricky started the car, and drove off in the opposite way from the Pawn Shop. "Hey, where you goin'…Twenty Third Street is the other way. " Quincy said.

"I'm takin' you home…I'm not lettin' you go anywhere with that dude." Quincy stared at Ricky with a disgusted look on his face. Ricky was right around the corner from Quincy's street.

"Hey…let me out right here. I will walk to my house from here." Ricky looked over at him and slowly pulled the car over. "Q…promise me you not goin' to go with him." Quincy opened the door with a sneaky smirk on his face. "Aight I'm not goin' to go with him…dang!" He shut the door and Ricky drove off. Once he was out of sight Quincy called Deon'te. "Hey, Deon'te change of plans… pick me on the corner of my street."

"Man, I was just 'bout to turn on Twenty Third," Deon'te complained.

"My bad." Deon'te hung up the phone. Quincy sat on the corner. While he was waiting he reached into his pocket and pulled out a pack of cigarettes and a lighter. Once he lit the cigarette, Deon'te's car pulled up quickly in front of him.

"Hurry up or we goin' be late," Deon'te said as he pushed open the car door. He quickly stood up and got in the car. Deon'te sped off and glared at Quincy. "Why did you change the pick up spot?"

"'Cause I was with Ricky and he didn't want me to come with you. He was gonna take me home so I told him to let me out and I was goin' to walk home."

"Why were you with him anyway...I told you all he's doin' is holdin' you back."

"I had some problems at home and I called him, so he could pick me up."

"You shoulda called me. I woulda came."

"He was the first one who came to my mind."

Deon'te reached in the back seat and picked up a book bag and tossed it into Quincy's lap. He looked inside it and there were about sixty sandwich bags filled with marijuana. "That's what we gonna take in," Deon'te said. Quincy closed the bag and threw it in the back before he threw his cigarette out the window.

"Oh! Let me tell you what I heard...that girl Shakia, the one you messed with at the party, is pregnant." Quincy eyes grew big, "Who told you that?" Deon'te chuckled, "I heard it through the grape vine."

"Man, seriously who told you that?"

"Jalissa...she told a lot of people."

"Did she say who the daddy was?" Quincy asked anxiously. "Naw she didn't know." Quincy banged his head on the dash board. "Calm down you actin' like you found out you the daddy!" Deon'te exclaimed. Quincy turned his head quickly, "I am!" Deon'te burst into laughter, "Oh snap you serious? How do you know?"

"I just know," Quincy replied anxiously. Deon'te continued to laugh uncontrollably. "Hee Hee Hell...that mess ain't funny!" Quincy exclaimed. Deon'te took a deep breath trying to control himself. "How far is this place?"

"Right at this corner," Deon'te answered. He pulled up beside a two-story building with boards in the windows and no front door. They got out of the car then leaned against the building. Deon'te pulled out his phone and dialed a number. "I'm here," he said. "Come down the hallway and I'm in the third door on the right." He hung up the phone and walked over to the car and grabbed the book bag from the back seat.

Before they went into the building, he turned to Quincy and said, "You have ya piece with you?" Quincy lifted his shirt showing him the gun. After he put his shirt down they crawled into the building through a large hole in one of the boards. Once they got inside, it was pitch black. They couldn't even see their hands. Deon'te handed the book bag to Quincy and then Quincy put it on his back. The boys tried to feel their way around the building until Deon'te reached into his back pocket and pulled out his cell phone. He pushed a button on his phone and it lit up. They used the light from the phone to guide them around the building. Finally Quincy saw a light shining under a door.

"There's a light," Quincy whispered. They walked towards the light and ended up in front of a closed door. Deon'te knocked twice before the door slowly opened. When the door opened there was no one in the doorway. Suddenly a man with a pistol peeked around the door.

"You're late," he said angrily. They slowly walked in and after they were in two more men came from behind the door. One of the men closed the door and the other posted against the wall.

"I thought you said you, were comin' alone," the man with the deep voice said.

"Oh…he's straight I wanted him to come with me," Deon'te replied. Quincy scanned the room and noticed there was an open window next to a broken chair.

The man with the deep voice said, "I'm Slim and that's my two killa's…that's all you need to know." Slim walked over to the window and stuck his head out and came back in with a large lunch box. When he opened it, he walked to Deon'te and showed him the money. Once he showed the money, Deon'te made his way to the window. Then he nodded at Quincy signaling him to show Slim the marijuana. He opened the bag and Slim reached in and pulled out a bag and nodded his head to the other men. He slid the money over to Deon'te and Quincy handed Slim the book bag. Suddenly Slim dropped the bag and pulled out a gun and a police badge.

"Freeze!" he yelled. Once Deon'te saw the badge, he jumped out of the window. The cop aimed at Deon'te but didn't shoot. Instead Slim jumped out of the window after Deon'te trying to catch him. Quincy tried to pull out his gun but the other two cops tackled him to the ground. One of the cops took his gun and slid it towards the wall. Quincy tried to fight his way free until three more cops burst through the door.

They all jumped on him and held him down. After they handcuffed him, a cop pressed his knee on Quincy's cheek and said, "You're under arrest for possession and distribution of illegal drugs."   …to be continued …

Abortion - Exodus 21:22-25
If men fight, and hurt a woman with child, so that she gives birth prematurely, yet no harm follows he shall surely be punished accordingly as the woman's husband imposes on him; and he shall pay as the judges determine. But if any harm follows, then you shall give life for life, eye for eye, tooth for tooth, hand for hand, foot for foot, burn for burn, wound, stripe for stripe.

This is only part one of a series of books on this subject matter by Mia N. Jones. If this book has impacted your life in anyway, you don't have to feel guilt or shame. Jesus died so that we would not have to bare the burden of guilt and shame of our mistakes. All you have to do is confess with your mouth Jesus as Lord over your life and believe in your heart that he died on the cross for your sins. This will open the door for God to erase all your shame. The next step would be to say this simple prayer out loud….

Dear God,

I know without Jesus I am lost… I believe your word…and your word says that if I confess with my mouth, The Lord Jesus and believe in my heart that God raised him from the dead, I shall be saved. I now invite you into my life and receive you, by faith. I am sorry for my sins, and I thank you for your forgiveness. I confess you now as my lord and savior; I am now a new creature in Christ, and a child of God. Thank you for saving me, now fill me with the Holy Spirit, so I can live the overcoming life, in Jesus' Name. Amen.

After saying this prayer be sure to join a Bible believing and teaching church, so you can learn and grow in the word of God.

Meet Author,

Mía N. Jones

Mía Jones, AKA "Bee", was born in Petersburg, Virginia where she lived until August of 1999. Later, she and her family moved to H-Town (Houston, Texas), where they joined the New Light Christian Center Church and learned the word of God under Pastors I.V. and Bridget Hilliard. After five years in Houston, the Jones family returned to Virginia.

Mía wrote her first book while in the third grade. Now sixteen, this dynamic young author continues to write and is completing the tenth grade. She enjoys playing basketball and volleyball—and don't get it twisted, she can school anybody in both.

Overall, Mía N. Jones is like any other teenager...she loves to talk on the phone, go out with friends, watch T.V. and <u>mostly</u>, serving the Lord.

PUBLIC APPEARANCES

Mia N. Jones is available for:

~ Speaking Engagements ~
~ Book Signings ~
~ Prayer Requests ~

To request Mia for your church, community
or organization's function, or for prayer
or consultation, please contact her:

via e-mail:
ChoicesMNJ@aol.com
or
authors@kingdompublishing.org

or
via postal mail:
P.O. Box 3715
Petersburg, VA 23205

Thank you for your interest.

For additional copies of "CHOICES"

please forward your check or money order
(plus shipping and handling) to:

Mia N. Jones
c/o CHOICES

P.O. Box 3715, Petersburg, VA 23205
(e-mail) ChoicesMNJ@aol.com
(web address) www.kingdompublishing.org

Qty.	Item	Unit Cost	Total
	CHOICES	11.95	
		Subtotal	
		Shipping	
		Grand Total	

<u>**SHIPPING & HANDLING:**</u> *Please add $2.00 shipping for each item ordered. For orders placed outside of the U.S., add $5.00 shipping per item.*

Ship to:

Organization: _____

_____   _____ **(Mr./Mrs./Ms.)**_____
Last Name   **First Name**

_____
Street Address

_____, _____ _____
City   **State**   **Zip**

Phone: (**)** _____   **E-mail:**_____

THANK YOU FOR PLACING YOUR ORDER!!!